COME ON CYMRU 2000!

New Football Writing from Wales

Keith Haynes

Published by Sigma Leisure – an imprint of
Sigma Press, 1 South Oak Lane, Wilmslow, Cheshire SK9 6AR, England.

British Library Cataloguing in Publication Data
A CIP record for this book is available from the British Library.

ISBN: 1-85058-729-9

Typesetting and Design by: Sigma Press, Wilmslow, Cheshire.

Cover Design: Sigma Press and MFP Design & Print

Cover photograph: Welsh Football Magazine

Photographs: by kind permission of the South Wales Evening Post, Colin Mansley, Wrexham Evening Leader, Gary Martin, Michael Morris, Welsh Football Magazine, Urban 75, Eric the Red, and Top Sport.

Printed by: MFP Design & Print

Foreword
– from Leighton James

Welcome to the new edition of *Come on Cymru!*. It is my great pleasure to be asked to introduce you to this excellent review of Welsh
soccer from the grass roots to the international scene.

Not for many years have we experienced such enthusiasm for the
national side and, despite recent setbacks, victories over Denmark
and Belarus have given great cause for optimism. Our clubs have had
varying degrees of success in the Nationwide League. Cardiff City's
promotion was definitely the highlight. Wrexham will be a little disappointed overall with their recent season and Swansea City will be
determined to go one better this time around. I would love to have
seen all three Welsh clubs in division two, but twelve months isn't so
long to wait. So come on Swansea!

The League of Wales continues to improve, albeit slower than had
been envisaged, and the lack of major sponsorship for our national
league is a great source of mystery for myself and many others.

Our schools' levels seem to be improving all the time due to the
very hard work of a dedicated bunch of teachers. Supported by their
parents our youngsters, with dedication, can reach the highest of levels – make no doubt about that.

On a personal note I am delighted with the quality of our younger
players, we have much to be proud about. They may well take a few
years to mature but I guarantee that some of them will most certainly
be the new Ryan Giggs or Mark Hughes.

Bobby Gould has relinquished his post as Wales national manager
– he tried his best and his efforts are to be congratulated. He as an individual could do no more and I wish him all the very best for the future. That leads me to this book and a new, up and coming author,
Keith Haynes. He writes with the passion we all have for the game in
Wales as do the many contributors in this book. I hope you enjoy this
excellent book as much as I have.

Good reading.

Leighton James

. . . and from Lloyd Aspin Jones:

This selection of football writing from Wales is the second offering from Keith Haynes, the editor and author of the first *Come on Cymru!* which appeared in November of 1998. For the second book some hard decisions had to be made. Do we publish a new book? Do we put out a revised book? Those who had already read the first offering would have felt cheated to read just a few new stories and the original ones in a 'new' book. With this in mind, Keith Haynes assembled the new stories, included in his very own identifiable style his own thoughts and sat back for a good read.

He was so impressed with the new breed of football writing which was clearly inspired by the first book he collected more, then more – and then some more. The upshot is *Come On Cymru 2000!* Keith decided to put out a whole new book of football stories and include updates from the original book. Of course with all these updates you just had to have some of the original stories too, it only made sense. So the reader wins – you get a load more pages.

After the deliberation came the test. Leighton James loved it and was delighted to offer his stamp of approval to the book. Many of Wales' best known writers also queued up to be included in the millennium edition of *Come on Cymru!* They could see that Keith had once again, even better – had exceeded far beyond expectations – and compiled and authored what can only be described as a bloody stormer of a book.

Nine months of hard graft is the result here in a book I honestly believe will not be equalled by any writer in any form for many years to come. But remember, Keith has not forgotten his roots, the terraces of Wales, where he learned more lessons than any classroom could teach, than any teacher could preach. He cajoled some, welcomed many, and satisfies us all here with a whacking great serving of Welsh football. The best of his first book and even better in the second. He has hit on a formula here and places his stake as one of Wales' best football writers. The new breed, call them what you want, they will have their say, from the graves of many fanzines come the opinions of tomorrow.

Buy the first book then settle back and drool over the second. I loved it and just know you will love it too.

Lloyd Aspin Jones

Thanks!

All the articles in this book are either written or edited by Keith Haynes. They do not represent any of the clubs named or the organisations that they work for.

All photographs are reproduced by kind permission of *The Wrexham Evening Leader, The South Wales Evening Post, Welsh Football* magazine or are the property of the editor of *Come on Cymru!* Many thanks to all those who assisted in collecting these photographs and for giving their permission to reproduce them in this book.

Keith Haynes would like to thank the following people for their assistance: Leighton James, Ian Williams, Jon Wilshire, John Burgum. Dave Lovett, Steve James, David Collins at Welsh Football magazine, The Swansea City Club Shop. Waterstones, Diff'rent Records, Urban 75, The Unofficial Barry Town internet page, The Welsh Books Council, Graham Beech and all at Sigma Press for their faith in me as a writer, all the contributors to both books (too numerous to mention) and, of course, the thousands of Welsh football fans who bought the first book, I hope you enjoy this edition as much as the first. Thank you for making it the success it was, it shows that Welsh football is anything but in the doldrums.

Have you got something to say?

Well say it then! Write to the author and editor of the Come on Cymru! books at

RANTO YANTO, PO BOX 19, GLOUCESTER, GL3 4YA

Include a SAE and send your story to the PO Box in Gloucester. Your story may be included in future editions of *Come on Cymru!*

The views of the individual are important, they may well not represent the club they follow or the official line that they take. This matters not – if you want to get your point or story across then put pen to paper or type your submission. If you wish you can include a photograph which will of course be returned.

Keith Haynes

For
Angela,
Sarah,
Victoria
and of course Dingle (a Super Furry Animal)

Contents

Chapter 1

Reasons to be Cheerful: Part Two

Keith Haynes

It was a pleasure to be involved in *Come on Cymru!*, which hit the streets in November 1998. The sales of the book soon made it apparent that a follow-up was needed as there were so many people with so many things to say. It didn't matter to me that some of the stories were from many years back or commented on the game in recent times, the fact remained that there is a massive support for the Welsh game. What I did find concerning was criticism from certain quarters of the topics included in the first book. Some identified, and rightly so, that the book did have more articles on Swansea City than, for example, Cardiff or Wrexham.

Well, what can I say? When compiling a book of this nature any good researcher will endeavour to make contact with as many folk as he can to get their views of their teams at the time. I contacted all the Welsh league clubs, their fanzines and magazines and hassled them on the Internet and telephone in the hope that some would get back and want to be included in the original book. Okay, some did, but the vast majority did not and their chance to have their say was lost. It seemed that they did not want to invest a small amount of time in a book written by Welsh football fans. Now it could be that they had neither the time nor the inclination to get involved and that's understandable. But having been given the chance to participate and declined, I believe they had no right to criticise the lack of exposure for the League of Wales or Wrexham FC for instance.

Am I wrong? Many had their chance to be included and, as far as I am concerned, still have one; this story is still unfolding and there is still room for more fireside tales and opinions on the game in Wales. It would be good to see more League of Wales clubs represented in the next book, can I make the point any clearer than that?

What is satisfying about being involved in a project like this is the bridge that can be built between supporters of opposing clubs, which gives a clearer understanding of where exactly they are coming from. Although not always welcomed, I participated on the Cardiff ISFA list (Internet collective for Cardiff City fans) for a few months and had many an interesting debate on the Welsh game. This resulted in Eric the Red's brilliant piece on the Ayatollah, an insight into how the Ayatollah became a part of the Cardiff City fans' way of introducing themselves to one another. When done *en masse*, of course, this is an incredible sight. Eric, I know, felt the first book was not so good as he hoped, but in my opinion he had room to criticise because at least he had bothered to get involved.

I learned a lot from doing the first book and I hope the experience has produced a more balanced view. If you don't agree, well at least you now know how you can change it. In the words of the famed John Lydon, "Get off your arses." Never a truer set of words has been spoken.

I wanted to include the Welsh media in this book so welcomed the views of sports writers and commentators. Here you will read their opinions on the game, as fans and as journalists. We all tune in to Radio Wales or whatever on a Saturday to hear their opinions on the game of the day, so it's right that they have some space here to further their views. Radio Wales has been a launch pad for many a sports presenter over the years: Radio 5 and Sky TV are littered with those who started their careers at Broadcasting House in Cardiff. You can tell that all of them keep an eye on the game in Wales whenever a Welsh side gets national publicity, it's hard to put your finger on it but you just know that deep down they are glowing with pride, no matter who is getting the headlines. In this book they get the chance to have their say.

The Internet, as I have already mentioned, is a vast web of opinions about Welsh football. Each of the Big Three has an ISFA list, a collection point for opinions about the clubs. It gives many hundreds of fans the opportunity to get involved in discussion and heated debate on the game, not always sensible, but then are any of us? The League of Wales has its own list which I found fascinating to read, it's such a shame that the invitation to be a part of this book has not been taken up.

I did sense an inferiority complex in these clubs at times, but this shouldn't be the case. Okay, I had a brief go at the league itself in the first book, but it has its place, I can't deny that, and a good crop of players is now setting the football league alight having started their playing days at Bangor City and Barry Town. Eifion Willimas, now a Torquay United player, is proof of this if anyone needed it. The real shame here is that the fans of Cardiff City and Swansea City urged their clubs to buy this talented player when he was available at a very small price. The clubs failed to see the blinding proof of this man's talents and he went for £70,000 to Torquay, their chairman can expect a massive return on his investment in the not too distant future. Marc Lloyd Williams, now at York City, and Tony Bird of Swansea have both maintained the standard set whilst in the League of Wales, further testament that this league should not feel inadequate.

It's true that the vast majority of football fans in Wales would not like to see their clubs in the League of Wales. I would hate to see Swansea City in this league, and to be honest I think the majority of Cardiff and Wrexham fans feel the same way. This is simply a fact, but, as I said, the league does have its place and the lower structure of the Welsh leagues has to be maintained for the very good players to have their chance in the football league itself, playing for Welsh clubs. That is, of course, if the powers that be at Swansea, Wrexham and Cardiff do not make the "Eifion" mistakes again. Cardiff City, of course, will say they haven't: Mark Delaney, now of Aston Villa and once of Carmarthen Town, earned the club a massive windfall when he transferred to Villa from Ninian Park. I really question here the commitment of Cardiff City to establishing themselves as a good First Division side in the near future when they sell on players of Delaney's calibre. Okay, he wasn't missed and Cardiff City won promotion to Division Two at the end of the 1998/99 season, but would he have been a crucial part of a promotion push in 2000? Time will tell.

But then Barry Town would argue that they are Wales's premier club. Their performances against Swansea and Cardiff in recent years have been memorable and who is to say that if they were a Third Division club they wouldn't win that league too? They are currently the FAW Premier Cup Champions, having defeated Wrexham in the final, which only goes to show that they are indeed a force in Welsh football.

Of course, you can't please everybody. The reviews of *Come on Cymru!* were favourable in some quarters and not so favourable in others. I sensed some jealousy amidst the real criticisms. I took it all on board, deciphered the rubbish, and got on with it. Sales were good, and over a thousand copies went in the first month. The responses I received from those who had bought the book were very positive indeed and some even took up the challenge of writing for this second volume. It was a pleasure to read their contributions and include them here for you to share.

So there you have it, another collection of football opinions from all walks of life and literally from all over the world. I have included some new photos and placed them in a more thoughtful way to complement the pieces they refer to. Enjoy it, hate it, and love it. But when you do finish reading, if you can transfer your thoughts to paper I would enjoy sharing them and who knows? One day a football fan in Brazil, Scotland or even in Wales may just want to say thank you, or even buy you a pint for sharing your reasons for standing, cheering, shouting and jeering in the name of your club.

Try it, but most of all enjoy it!

Chapter 2

Oh, what a luverly season: an epitaph to the 20th century

Keith Haynes

The 1998/99 football season in Wales finished with Cardiff City back in Division 2 and Swansea City faltering at the last hurdle in the play-offs. Wrexham recovered from a desperate run to regain Division 2 status and Barry Town yet again won the League of Wales title. They also won the FAW Premier Cup. Inter CableTel (now Inter Cardiff) will represent Wales in Europe after winning the Welsh Cup. Cwmbran & Aberystwyth share the limelight in the new European competition too. All in all only Cardiff achieved what they set out to do. Barry Town were bankers and Swansea City did exactly what the majority of supporters felt they would, absolutely nothing.

It's very hard to explain the feeling you get when you are standing in a seated away end in Scunthorpe at half past ten on a summer's evening and the season has come to an abrupt end. I should have known better than believe John Hollins when he said his squad was good enough to win promotion. Even though there were glaring omissions in midfield and up front when we were badly hit by injury and suspensions in January, February and March, I had spoken to many Swans fans who said, "You have to give John a chance, he knows what he is doing." Well, you have to admire his commitment to his squad, but at the end of the day it all went down the pan. Bad defending and a failure to take a string of chances were the reasons at Scunthorpe, but the season lasts 46 games not the last two. We had been filled with false hope and I should have known.

My feelings at this time were of anger towards the owners of the club for not insisting that the funds that they said were available were given to John Hollins. I had travelled thousands of miles in pursuit of promotion and watched some appalling games of football, the fact we made it in to the play-offs was a miracle in itself, a testament to the worst league I had seen in all the time I had been watching football. Like thousands of other Swansea fans, I had been kicked in the rare bits yet again.

So who do you blame? In Swansea's case the blame initially lies with the players and the management. But as is usual at Swansea, it goes deeper than this. The club has a visionary Vice-Chairman and owner in Neil McClure, but his stories of ground moves and investment are wearing thin. So thin, in fact, that this season, the first of the millennium, may well be a watershed for McClure and his board – who continue to talk of business plans and investment. But all it is at this time is talk. The local council await the next business plan and I get the feeling they are getting a little bit tired of waiting; things have to move on, and two years of talking gets boring even for the most patient of people. Time will tell if Neil McClure can deliver the ground that he continues to talk about on a daily basis. If he does I will be the first to shake his hand and give him the praise he deserves for securing such a daring move; if he doesn't this season could, I fear, be his last.

The Swans FA Cup run was magnificent and many thousands witnessed defeats of Millwall (3-0), Stoke City (1-0) and then West Ham

(1-0), who they held to a draw at Upton Park. That night at The Vetch when an injured Martin Thomas hammered home the winner from outside the area will live long in the memory. It was a marvellous achievement by the team and, of course, the manager, who had turned around the Swansea squad from deadbeats to FA Cup giant-killers. A magnificent achievement, a marvellous achievement, call it what you like, I thought it was the mutt's nuts of games. They were defeated 1-0 at home by Derby County in the next round but the damage had been done. Swansea City are now the only Third Division side to ever knock out a Premiership side in the FA Cup.

The cup campaign brought about a number of injuries that the club amazingly failed to address. These injuries and suspensions meant that the Swans often fielded sides eight players adrift of the side that knocked West Ham out of the FA Cup. It wouldn't be until the last game of the season that we would see the same side again – convincing proof that the club had failed to strengthen the squad when so many could see it was weak. The reasons (no other explanations having been offered) are simple, either the manager was so stubborn (or loyal) that he wouldn't do it or the club had no cash available and John Hollins knew this so he got on with the job. There are times when clubs have to be honest with the fans and here the club earned no brownie points at all for failing to answer the key question – why is this being allowed to happen?

I find it difficult to have faith in anyone who talks in millions about property development yet can't spend thousands to strengthen a squad that could then earn them so much more. Once again the fans are the ones who are left asking the questions, once again there are no answers apart from shrugged shoulders and clenched fists, symbols from a manager that will also wear thin if he fails to achieve promotion this season.

John Hollins has done remarkably well with the players he has. The Swansea supporters recognise this and honour him by chanting his name at every game the team plays. I agree he has done well, but failure is failure. I just hope that John Hollins addresses the problems that are there for all to see and sweeps us off our feet in 2000. Neil McClure should follow this example and turn his words into actions. On the former I have hope, on the latter, well you have to smile until you see bricks and mortar being laid. Plans for a rock concert at a venue that should be prepared for football in a few months are not welcome. This year's fad in thrashing guitars should be playing elsewhere whilst our new pitch is being laid. I fear the winter of 1999 and spring of 2000 will be upon us before we really know if Neil McClure is the visionary he would have us all believe he is. Let's not forget that he has a massive task on his hands and one that requires real money. I will be only too pleased to sing his praises in any subsequent book if he is successful so go on, Neil, make our day. But first please realise that a 25,000 all-seater stadium won't be full in the Third Division.

John Hollins, passionately admired at Swansea City.

Apparently, lengthy discussions brought about the return of Frank Burrows to Ninian Park in 1998. I am all too aware that many Cardiff City supporters viewed his return sceptically, the old adage of "Never to return" was being quoted by many. But return he did and set about reforming a City side that had had little TLC over the previous few seasons. Frank packed in a very rewarding job at The Academy of Football at West Ham before returning to Cardiff, but this time it was on his terms.

Frank Burrows is famed for his dressing room outbursts and many stories are told by ex-players who have been on the receiving end of his lengthy tirades regards their performance. It seems the man has not changed too much since he last led a Cardiff City side to promotion but he did have the backing of the board and he set about forming a squad of players that eventually gained promotion to the Second Division. At some stages it looked like he might even win the title – a superb performance from a man who had taken a massive gamble by returning to Ninian Park!

He brought in players he knew could do a job for him such as ex-Swansea players Jason Bowen and Andy Legg. John Williams, who is constantly referred to as "the flying postman", led the Cardiff front line with Kevin Nugent, and how they prospered. Never once looking as if they would fail, the Cardiff City side of 1999 booked their play-off place by the end of Easter and gained promotion in front of thousands at Ninian during the last few weeks of the season. Frankie had returned! And he even made the club a massive windfall by selling Mark Delaney to Aston Villa. If nothing else, Frank has a shrewd eye for a good player and a bargain buy, he has proved it constantly over the years at Cardiff and Swansea.

Other significant improvements brought about by Burrows were the appointments of Colin Pascoe and Mike Davenport, both of whom had served with him at previous clubs. Once again Frank stuck with what he knew to forge a back-room staff he could trust. He worked with those he knew and Cardiff City gained promotion.

Frank Burrows doesn't deal in myths and fantasies, he is a straight talking manager who wears his heart on his sleeve, an achiever at the lower end of the football league. If something is wrong he will tell the club's owners; if it's not addressed the press find out. He was quoted as saying that he did not want his Cardiff side of 1999 torn apart because the club wanted to make money, he wanted his side to remain intact so City could have a good go at the Second Division. He got his way, he got the support of the fans and the turn of the century is looking good for the canny Scotsman who has such an impressive knowledge of lower league football. His only mistake has to be not signing Eifion Williams from Barry Town just a few miles down the road. City fans will forgive him for this if the team fulfil their ambitions in 2000.

Samesh Kumar has stepped to one side for now, I suspect that he realises that Cardiff City will need another leader at the helm for their assault on the Second Division. Kumar talks well and presents a positive image from Ninian Park. I really believe that they will succeed providing the board supports Frank Burrows and remains stable whilst he leads the team forward.

The Cardiff City squad is also looking good. The reserve team keeper, Seamus Kelly, stood in for first team regular John Hallworth and acquitted magnificently as Cardiff defeated Southend at Roots Hall towards the end of the season. Jason Fowler, the reformed Legg and Bowen and the ever-dangerous Kevin Nugent will, I believe, be irrepressible in the Second Division. Legg and Bowen were discarded by Reading in humiliating circumstances and will go back there this season with one big point to prove. It is certain that they will do so. Danny Hill is another who is now finding his feet. Danny signed from Spurs and can come off the subs' bench and tear defences apart. He is a real bargain.

So all is looking rosy for City, but it can change. Frank has been relatively unsuccessful outside the Third Division, with brief exceptions at Swansea and Portsmouth. He, too, hits a major hurdle and I

Things are looking brighter for Cardiff City as they take on the Second Division

for one just know that this time he will clear it easily. But he has to have the board's support. If he does, Cardiff City will figure in the play-offs for the Second Division come May 2000.

Wrexham have had Bryan Flynn at the helm since God invented grass. He cleverly brought in Ian Rush at the start of the season so he could learn the ropes in the right way at The Racecourse. Rush just couldn't find the net in the league and although he has now left Wrexham, the club will reap the benefits of having such a high profile player in the squad this season. Wrexham stumbled so badly towards the end of the season that many had them down for a return to the Third Division and local sports writers were very concerned that Flynn had been at the club for too long. True to tradition, he turned the club around and Wrexham retained their Second Division status with games to spare.

The fans on the other hand would not have minded if Flynn had departed the club, the general feeling was that he had been there for too long, he needed to step aside for another manager. Flynn has flirted with promotion on many occasions whilst at The Racecourse and this season could also be a watershed for him if he fails to achieve. The club's chairman sounds like a man happy with his lot; Flynn has made him a lot of money in transfers and the team came close to a Wembley appearance in the Autowindscreen Trophy. Perhaps this saved Flynn from a premature departure. On deadline day

Wrexham 1999, failed to achieve, but will always figure as long as Flynn is the man in charge.

he showed again that he is the sort of manager that Chairmen love. He went out and secured good quality youngsters from Man United and Newcastle who will figure prominently this season. I believe that Wrexham too will not be far away from the play-offs come May.

It's warm now and the thud of leather on willow is soothing. The big three have much work to do, Welsh football needs them all to succeed to continue the rebirth of the game in Wales. Swansea will succeed and so will Cardiff and Wrexham. I have to say this because it needs to happen.

The national side has put in excellent performances of late, but having been there so many times before I get the feeling that once again they will fail. I hope not, but I think the structure of the game has a long way to go. Bobby Gould has gone, but he was never going to stick around after it was clear the majority of fans did not want him as manager. If Wales had been successful while Gould was the team manager then so be it. I would have settled for that. He was obscure at times as Robbie Savage and Nathan Blake demonstrate, but he was passionate and wanted to succeed. The next manager to lead a successful national side will produce such massive gates at club level that maybe even McClure's dream of a 25,000-seat stadium in Swansea will become reality. Maybe Mark Hughes is the man?

Mark Hughes – new Wales manager

The week after Gould hung up his growling tracksuit I received this contribution about the Italian job from **Paul Thomas** of Newport.

I went to Bologna with a few mates, we went at the last moment once we found out that getting tickets was easy and wouldn't cause us a problem. Having watched Cardiff City for most of the season, and what a season it was, I was full of anticipation when making the 3-hour trip by plane to see Wales play. We arrived on the Friday afternoon and already hundreds of fellow Welshmen were entertaining the locals with songs about our heritage, including anti-Swan songs from a few idiots. But that was soon put in its place. A big gang of Cardiff lads with a few Jacks in tow, all mates, put these idiots to the sword and off they went, tails between their legs. It was now Wales United, the way it should be.

We spent the afternoon drinking and making friends. I didn't see any trouble and felt quite at ease with the police and locals, it was a great trip. On the Saturday we went for a few drinks with some Wrexham lads from Mold and a few Swansea lads, we were expecting a draw at the least. One local said we would lose 4-0 and laughed at our optimism. I should have listened to him.

In the ground we found we had a good view of the pitch. There was no hassle, well, not too much, and the local beer had filled me with optimism. But when the game started the team was totally pathetic. All of the players were clueless and showed no bottle at all. We were 1-0 down in five minutes and then another. Before half-time it was 3-0 to the Italians, and they hadn't even slipped into second gear.

We chanted and sang as the Italians made victory signs to us. Then it was Gould's turn – he had to go. "We want Bobby out. We want Bobby out." The wolf-headed man looked over and growled, we returned V-signs and continued barracking him. We lost 4-0, it was humiliating.

After the game the Italians thought they would have a go at us, chanting "England" and similar abuse. What a pathetic thing to do! They got the reaction they wanted, and for the first time things were a bit hostile, but I wasn't surprised. They should have known better.

Anyway, we went home to the news that Gould had gone, the big-

Bye Bye Bobby, another Welsh manager bites the dust and leaves with no consideration for timing.

gest cheer of the trip I can tell you. It leaves us yet again in the shite when it comes to a guiding light, but at least we won't have Gould licking us with his eyebrows again. There is at least that to be thankful about.

Paul Thomas

Well said, Paul. Gould couldn't take the pressure and went. The fans, the only ones who really care, were instrumental in this. The Manics were right, so were the fans. It's a shame he left it so long.

For the present, whilst Barry Town win what's important and the other three flirt with success at a low level, reality is something everyone involved in Welsh football needs to get a grip with. Since the publication of *Come on Cymru!* things have improved. I hope that soon we have a Welsh side back in the First Division, and to be quite frank I couldn't care what colours they play in as long as Wales gets the plaudits and the game improves throughout the country.

It's down to a few wise men and a few dreamers. We all know who they are and I wish them all the best. My message to Swansea, Cardiff, Wrexham, Barry Town, Aberystwyth Town and, yes, even Inter CableTel is, 'Get out there and do it for Wales.' Let's get behind them all and leave the divisions of stupidity behind. The terraces could be packed with hope in a year's time and I want to see them packed with smiling faces too, no matter where those faces come from.

Come on Cymru!

Chapter 3

They'll be Dancing in the Streets of Inter CableTel

Keith Haynes and Mario Reece

The League of Wales has given clubs that otherwise wouldn't have the chance to do so the chance to represent Wales in Europe. The editor decided to test out the depth of feeling for the game in Wales and put in an appearance at the 1999 Welsh Cup final. It was exciting, well, the last few kicks were exciting, and the crowd of well over 1,000 loved it.

Welsh Cup finals, eh? They used to be played the day after the FA Cup final, more often than not on a Sunday and with a questionable attendance figure printed the next day in the press. My last journey to a Welsh Cup final was in the early nineties, Swansea City v Wrexham at Cardiff Arms Park. It was a blistering day. All the Swans fans seemed to be wearing the hooped black and white away top which looked great on the TV and the Wrexham lads on the opposite side of the ground sang in patches and made the whole event like a Wales away game. My point concerning the attendance here is that it was supposedly 5,000. I don't think so! The whole of one side of the Arms Park was packed with Swansea fans on the lower tier and many hundreds were above them. Wrexham on the other side had a good following of at least 3,000. So 5,000? Yes, in ticket sales maybe, but I, like the majority, bought my ticket on the day of the game, at the gate. The estimated attendance that day was 11,000. Mm?

The 1999 final was held at Penydarren Park, the home of Merthyr Tydfil, an interesting ground that I have attended on many occasions for obscure third-round Welsh Cup ties on Wednesday nights in the past. It was fitting that the game should be held there, after all Merthyr are not in the League of Wales and have fought tooth and nail not be in the league, preferring to make their way in the English pyramid system. So the Welsh FA choose Merthyr? Interesting.

Before...

I managed a few beers prior to the game and recognised many faces from the North Bank at Swansea. These, of course, were the supporters of Carmarthen Town, approximately 800 souls from West Wales seemingly 90 minutes from a remarkable European adventure. I, for one, really felt that they could do it. Thankfully, Carmarthen had turned out in force to cheer their local team on. I had trained with the team as a youngster, before they made the big step up to greatness in the League of Wales. Back then they were no force at all, now, it seemed, they had reached their pinnacle and a Welsh Cup final was to be the icing on the cake.

It was good to see the fans mingling together as they do at Wembley for the "other final", there seemed to be no animosity at all. I have witnessed some nasty moments at Merthyr when Cardiff City supporters attend Swansea v Merthyr games in pursuit of their wish to prove that they are the best in Wales – not that they ever do. The Cardiff City fans I know regard these people as scum. We all have them, and like all scum they often float to the top, ruining games and bringing our teams and clubs into disrepute. They were not evident on this day, a day when it seemed their wish to meet with Swansea City fans could easily have been achieved. Very odd, maybe they are not aware of Carmarthen's location in West Wales and the fact that many Swans fans live there. It seemed obvious to me that they would travel to the game to cheer on Carmarthen Town, but maybe the knuckleheads are just that.

I enjoyed the atmosphere and was surprised that many were disappointed with the attendance. The Inter supporters had turned out a good 500 and this plus Carmarthen's turnout made the game a great advert for the two clubs. I spoke to one chap, an Inter supporter (and Cardiff City), who expected to see the ground full and was amazed that so few had turned up for the game. He revelled in the opportunity of telling me about Celtic's visit to the capital a few years earlier when Inter played the Scottish Cup winners in a game at Ninian Park.

"Should have won that night," he kept saying. From what I can remember Inter were soundly beaten but did themselves proud. I pointed out to him that from the clubs in the League of Wales only

Barry Town, in my humble opinion, were capable of beating a league side.

"Bollocks," he replied. "Barry Town are shite, they are nothing without Eifion Williams. You see next year when they struggle." Surely not? I pointed out to him that Barry had sold their best goalscorers of recent seasons in Eifion, Tony Bird and Dave O. Gorman and had still managed to win the league hands down.

"Ah, but where are the bastards today?" he said. "Probably enjoying their summer holidays, mate," I replied. "Barry are rubbish," he shouted. We were going around in circles, and I was not getting anywhere. It seems Barry Town are the Man United of Wales in League of Wales terms, hated by many just because they have success on their side.

My mate Mr Inter wobbled off pontificating about "the bastards" and I never saw him again. Football eh? Brings all sorts together. Odd thing here is that I know quite a few Barry Town supporters who follow Cardiff City and, of course, the same could be said of some of Inter CableTel's following. So are they really bastards, or just when it suits?

The Game

It's often said that these games are watched by one man and his dog. Well, over a thousand men and women and, yes, two dogs watched this final, a game that was clearly played between two teams who were nervous of the potential prize – European footy and all.

I'm not going to give you a blow-by-blow account but after the final whistle it still hadn't been resolved. Penalties decided it and Inter CableTel won the game. Carmarthen, I felt, edged it if there was to be a winner in real play. They scored a good goal in extra time. I missed Inter's effort. They lifted the trophy and ran about a bit. Their defender ran more with the trophy than he did throughout the game. They looked like Hereford United, maybe it was the shirts. Paul Evans, Inter's captain, was crying, Gary Wager was a hero and George Wood the manager drank a crate of beer. The suits from the FAW clapped and smiled, clearly happy that their non-event had gone off without trouble. You can always spot them: black-suited men who smell of wine and with a woman or two in tow.

From the top: Paul Evans collects the Welsh Cup . . . and for the first time take on Glasgow Celtic in a European competition.

I can't slag off the supporters who were there, or the teams. It meant loads to many who were there, much more than it meant to me. I was only there as an observer, merely watching and trying to get a flavour of the football final of Wales. Maybe if Barry Town had been there it would have been better, more atmosphere to taunt the Carmarthen following. I don't know. I left a little bit bored. I did, though, feel content. I felt that Swansea, Cardiff and Wrexham were in the right league and the rebels were right to be just that. Rebels.

Afterwards...

Travelling home I smiled a lot, my mate was talking of potential play-off places and such. We passed the Inter coach on the carriageway down to the M4. The players were singing and I saw the cup again, or was it another team from another final even less publicised than this one? The Schweppes Rabbiting Final of Mid Wales perhaps? Possibly as interesting to those it matters to. Possibly.

The Welsh Cup final passed off in a five-minute spell of excitement that all penalty shoot-outs bring. I liked that bit. My mate did too, he thought it was funny. I now know what it's like for an alien to land on the planet and witness a game (football) with no knowledge of the passion that keeps it alive. I spared a thought, too, for Robbie James, who came into my thoughts for some strange reason or other.

We stopped at a service station on the M4 going east and I saw a Carmarthen Town supporter with his son, supping a cup of tea. Their shirts seemed old and shoddy. "Not that bad mate," I said.

"Nah," he replied. "I don't really care, it was a bit crap really." I asked him where he was heading. "Ipswich," he replied. Our topic of conversation turned once again to the play-offs. He was an avid Ipswich Town fan of 25 years, but born in Carmarthen. He had no current connections there apart from that. I asked him jokingly how he found out about the final and that Carmarthen were playing. He told me he got to see them whenever he could, when Ipswich were not playing that is. "Do you know what I mean?" he said.

Sadly, I did. We said our goodbyes and I easily spotted his car in the car park. Ipswich Town stickers on the back etc... The words "second-best" sprung to mind. The final was full of fans who supported other teams, teams that probably meant more to them than the sides playing. It's a shame that the Welsh Cup final should be like this but that's the way it is. I wish Inter CableTel well in Europe, they will need a lot of luck.

It's never going to be the same again the Welsh Cup final, never. Don't blame anyone, and if you do genuinely support a League of Wales side, don't for God's sake settle for second best. A thousand folk and two dogs can't be wrong.

Postscript: Three weeks after the Welsh Cup final Barry Town once again triumphed in the FAW Cup, an invitation trophy contested by the Football League sides and various Welsh League sides. Barry Town beat Wrexham, thus proving my point that they are, indeed, the best side in Wales, even when pitted against the likes of Swansea, Wrexham and Cardiff. It's just a shame that some of their supporters can't be bothered to write about their successes of recent years. Maybe next time?

Chapter 4

Welsh Football Fans on the Internet

The three Welsh league clubs have an abundance of web sites to choose from and the best of these are represented here. Gary, Rhys and Michael have spent a number of years fine-tuning their sites to a very professional standard and the fans of these clubs now go there first to find out exactly what is happening.

I personally stumbled across the Internet way of life by mistake. I'm not saying I wouldn't have found it eventually, but four years ago there seemed to be little choice if you wanted news on your club. Now you can read about the vast majority of the clubs in Wales today, even my home town club of Haverfordwest County has leapt into the new age of the World Wide Web.

Many thousands of Welsh football fans from all over the world browse the pages of the three sites featured here. I believe that Gary Martin will reach 100,000 hits over the next twelve months. The clubs are not too keen on their secrets being discussed on the Internet but it happens, and long may it continue. The stifling attitude of some clubs to their fans opinions is disgraceful. These clubs must realise that debate actually strengthens football in the UK. Their threats of banishment and the like will do nothing to enhance the relationship between football fans and the owners of these clubs.

Did you know that one club owner feeds his daily Internet habit by sending messages to the fans, not always nice ones either? Another chairman gets members of his family to spy on certain sites and send him copies of what is being said. And it's not powerful, eh?

The sites were started by the fans and are being run by the fans so the tottering towers of insanity can read and moan all they like. Not even the most powerful chairman in the land can abolish them. That's a fact.

In Wales you have official sites, unofficial sites, which are the best by far, and even supporters' groups have their own web sites. They offer opinions they offer arguments and they offer friendship. And I have to say that some of the writers, such as Mouthful of Lead's Anthony Thomas, are so effective with the written word that it frightens these club owners to death. That's the point, that's the reason why it's so vital that this forum remains. And it's bloody funny too!

The contributors to this chapter (Rhys Gwynllyw, of Webbed Robin fame; Michael Morris, the brains behind Cardiff City On Line, one of the best sites in the country; and Gary Martin of the unofficial Swansea site) have transformed the Internet for Welsh football fans throughout the world.

A Swansea City View

Gary Martin – http://www.scfc.co.uk

Let's get the booing and hissing out of the way right now – I am a Maths teacher and have been since 1973. Around the mid-80s when computers and related subjects started appearing on schools' curricula, a simplistic solution for many head teachers was to assume that people like myself would be the ideal ones to involve in their teaching – and so my interest in computing began. I must confess, I have never found computers themselves to be very interesting – but the versatility and speed that they lent to various tasks, I found fascinating.

The Internet has been around since the early 80s, but it was always a very user-unfriendly medium and surrounded by mystery – until the latter half of this decade. Instead of having to memorise a series of complicated keystrokes to achieve even the simplest task, a "point-and-click-on-a-picture approach" soon increased its appeal.

It wasn't until December 1995 that I first poked my toe into the murky cyber-pond that is the Internet, but since that time I have been hooked. Apart from the usual thing that men first tend to look at on the Internet – fishing sites, cars, woolly cardigans etc. – I soon started to search for football-related sites. Imagine my dismay when I found only a handful of Premiership sites and even fewer for the other divisions' clubs.

This prompted me to try and create a Swansea City site. But where would I start? To create even the simplest web page required knowledge of HTML – a coding language that isn't at all complicated, but at first glance appears harder than Hebrew. Wales was not without representation in cyberspace, even at this early time. And so it was to a fellow countryman, Rhys Gwynllyw, who had a Wrexham site on the net, that I turned.

At the time, Rhys was a student at Aberystwyth University and was making use of his free university Internet access to further the cause of the Robins. He proved to be most helpful and I am pleased to be able to say that I have been able to do the same for others as my knowledge has increased.

My first few attempts at a site hit all sorts of snags – mainly because my chief adviser was used to a system at university that was different from the ones found in the commercial world. Anyway, all was soon resolved and the Swans first appeared on the Internet on the 20th January 1996. The site has come a long way since that time and has now built up quite a large following from Jacks in all parts of the globe. It is also used as a resource by journalists, who find the detailed records gathered together in one place a boon when preparing background material for a story or an interview.

Living in Wales and close to the action, we probably take it for granted that we can get the latest news from Teletext, Welsh radio, TV and even the local paper. But imagine someone in Russia, Sydney or Caracas (yes, they're all places from which Jacks regularly check the site). Through the Internet they can get the latest news at the same time as we do, albeit it in a different time zone. Did you know that you can read the Western Mail in Patagonia on the same day that it comes out in Cardiff thanks to the Internet? Why, you even get to see the colour pictures!

So by checking the site, anyone with Internet access can see the latest scores, read the match reports, view the goals on video and even listen to the chants on the North Bank just hours after the match has ended - whether they are in Cwmtwrch or Kathmandu.

Apart from the Football League clubs in Wales, lots of other clubs now have a presence on the web – even some local league parks' teams. I try to maintain an up-to-date list of links to football sites in Wales so you can always check http://www.scfc.co.uk to see if the team that you are interested in is on-line yet.

What have I got out of creating and maintaining the site? Well, quite a lot. I have met people from all parts of the world and have made many good friends. I can't recall the number of offers of hospitality that I've received – and as one of my hobbies is foreign travel, I have even taken advantage of some of them. One such offer saw me guesting for an over-40s team, the Gainesville Immortals (Florida), one Tuesday evening with temperatures in the 90s – Mr Mad or what?

An integral part of a thriving web site is its mailing list. We have been very fortunate at Swansea to have had a particularly active one from the outset and I know that expats getting up for work in all corners of the world rush straight to their computers for their daily fix of Swans news and banter before doing anything else. Many of these people have never set eyes on each other, but through the list's interaction they regard each other as good friends. The articulate and thought-provoking postings on the list have even influenced the club into putting some of the issues raised on their agenda.

One of the most enjoyable things about the mailing list for me is actually meeting these "e-mail addresses" face to face at home and away games. In fact, the interest was so great that we have produced our own merchandise complete with logo.

As I write this, at the end of the 20th century, it would be foolish to try and predict what the future holds for soccer fans on the Internet, as you are already in the future if you are reading this! What I will say, though, is that the leaps in technology witnessed in just the last three years that my Swansea site has been in existence have been phenomenal. Who would have thought that it would be commonplace to download a single file that less than five years ago wouldn't have been able to fit on your hard drive.

No matter what the future holds for the Internet, it is certain that football clubs and their fans would be well advised to be involved.

The Webbed Robin

Rhys Gwynllyw – http://come.to/webbedrobin

I created The Webbed Robin in 1995, whilst working as a researcher in the Department of Mathematics at the University of Wales, Aberystwyth. It was there that I first encountered the Internet and naturally subscribed to e-mailing lists relating to Computational Fluid Dynamics and the like! However, I had my fair share of subscriptions to football-related sites too.

In March 1995 an e-mail was sent to a general football mailing list enquiring whether any Wrexham supporters existed on the Internet and I replied to the message. The e-mail was from Steven Rubio, a Californian who became a Wrexham supporter simply through reading the book *Twenty-Two Foreigners in Funny Shorts*! (full details at the end of this section).

Being a sports enthusiast, Steven bought the book, which was intended for the American market, as a guide to the 1994 World Cup hosted in that country. The book, written by Pete Davies, includes the basics of the game, the history of the World Cup and fundamental tactics employed by different nations. What made the book different from all the others on a similar theme was that it also conveyed to the reader the passion that this greatest of all games can generate. To do this Pete chronicled the 1992/93 promotion season of his favourite football club – the mighty Wrexham AFC.

Following correspondence with Steven Rubio, we decided to take advantage of the computing facilities supplied by our respective universities in order to supply a service to Wrexham supporters with access to the Internet. Steven organised the Wrexham e-mailing list, based at the University of California, Berkeley, enabling Wrexham supporters to communicate with each other. I decided to set up Wrexham AFC's first World Wide Web site dedicated to the cause!

Four years on, the e-mailing list and the Wrexham web site are both going strong – the mailing list currently has 310 members from all over the world.

My Wrexham web site remained nameless for almost a year before it was finally baptised. The drive home to Aberystwyth following a 0-4 humiliation at the Goldstone Ground, Brighton gave my (now) wife and I plenty of time to think of a name. Anything to take our minds off a pretty dismal display. Eventually we came up with the name "Webbed Robin" after we had passed a couple of duck ponds in Dorset (honest).

Despite a number of changes in the Webbed Robin, the aims of the web site have remained the same. These are to keep the Wrexham supporter informed of what's happening at the Racecourse and to promote the club. Information takes the form of regular match reports and news coverage, whilst promoting the club includes supplying the visiting supporter with as much relevant information as possible and having the merchandising catalogue on-line. Whilst most of the work to keep the site up to date is done by myself, the Webbed Robin benefits from the great assistance given by other Wrexham supporters keen to keep the service on-line.

Why, one may ask, do I do it? Let me detail my early years supporting the Robins as these formed the foundation of my passion.

I was born in the maternity ward of Wrexham Maelor hospital which, I'm proud to say, is only a stone's throw away from the Racecourse. My grandfather supported Wrexham for 65 years and it was he who introduced me to the delights of watching Wrexham on the football field. Well, the delights came later in life as my first game was a goal-less draw against Aldershot in April 1974. The Wrexham team for that match included Mickey Thomas, David Smallman and Eddie May.

Most of my formative years were spent in Y Bala, some thirty miles away from Wrexham. With all due respects to Bala Town, the draw of events at Y Cae Ras was stronger than that from Maes Tegid. Getting to Wrexham from Y Bala was not the easiest in those days. If car transport were not available we would have to resort to the delights of the Crossville Omnibus Company. This would result in the choice of either missing the last 15 minutes of the match or hanging around the streets of Wrexham for a couple of hours, waiting for the last bus to Barmouth. Not ideal for a 14-year-old, but at least we got back in time for "Match of the Day", just.

I got hooked on Wrexham during the 1976/77 season in which we missed promotion to the (old) Second Division by a whisker. Our final match of that season, at home to champions Mansfield, remained for twenty years my most disappointing match ever. Unlike our 1995 FA Cup quarter-final defeat at Saltergate, the Mansfield scar took only a year to heal and what a year that was. The 1977/78 season remains Wrexham's greatest, in which we won the (old) Third Division championship, won the Welsh Cup and reached the quarter-finals of both the FA Cup and the Football League Cup. It was a season I will never forget, a season that saw the Racecourse entertain crowds in excess of 19,000 on no less than six occasions.

In that championship season we gained promotion by tonking Rotherham United seven goals to one. All I remember of that match was that I was one of only a handful of supporters that didn't manage to make it onto the pitch after the game – my dad wouldn't let me! I've since forgiven him, but in my 25 years of supporting Wrexham I have not yet trod on the Racecourse turf. Maybe I'll wait until I'm ashes!

My most abiding memory of that season was the match in which we won the championship, which was also my first Wrexham match away from the Racecourse. There will always be a piece of my heart at Edgar Street, Hereford. It wasn't the best game – a goal each with Mickey Thomas scoring the equaliser – but the atmosphere was electric and I was such a proud member of the 6,000 strong travelling army. I did make it onto the pitch that time.

These days the reason for my support has possibly changed although it's still as passionate. Now that I live and work in Bristol the only expression of my roots is to follow the Robins on their quest for glory: week-in, week-out; home and away. Being computer literate it seemed natural to convert my daily dose of Wrexham news to the hard disk and onward to the virtual world. It may be sad, but Wrexham are my team and I love them.

The Webbed Robin could not possibly exist without the support of my wife Karen, who is also a Wrexham season ticket holder. Indeed, I'm writing this part of the article on my laptop as she's driving the two of us from our home in Bristol to watch Wrexham entertain Oldham Athletic. It's no surprise that Karen caught the Wrexham bug as her first ever football match happened to be one of Wrexham's greatest ever performances. On January 4th 1992, Wrexham, having finished bottom of the entire Football League the previous season, played current champions Arsenal in the third round of the FA Cup. Wrexham's 2-1 victory was one of the biggest shock results in the history of the most famous of cup competitions. Karen was impressed!

Her next match was the fourth round of the cup, at the Boleyn Ground, Upton Park. A fantastic battling display against West Ham United sealed Karen's allegiance to the Mighty Robins.

Some people think that we take things a bit too far in supporting Wrexham. There were raised eyebrows when the date of our wedding was switched from a Saturday to a Friday so that we could go and watch the football at the weekend. It was a lovely wedding but our plans for watching the match were a comedy of errors. Basically, we didn't get to see it.

The first day of our honeymoon was supposed to be at Boundary Park, Oldham. The next week was to be spent in Rome and hence we booked flights from Manchester Airport for the Sunday. All this had been done well in advance of the fixture – forgetting that the date coincided with the third round of the cup. With Wrexham's cup pedigree we really should have expected the Oldham fixture to be postponed. The draw for the third round came – Wrexham away to Wimbledon. With Crystal Palace, sharing Selhurst Park with the Dons, also drawn to play there, the Wrexham match was switched to the Sunday. It left us with the choice of watching the game or flying to Rome and I'm afraid to say that we let Wrexham down and opted for the flight. Whilst in Rome we did as the Romans do and watched Roma play Lazio at the Olympic Stadium in the quarter-finals of the Copa Italia.

Unfortunately, the days of Wrexham playing in Europe are currently in the past due to those Welsh clubs playing within the English leagues not being allowed to compete in the Welsh Cup. This ban followed UEFA's decision that such "exiled" clubs could not represent their nation in the European Cup Winners' Cup. The introduction of this rule was a sad day for Welsh football. Not because the standard of Welsh football in Europe would necessarily drop, the League of Wales clubs have represented Wales with pride and passion in those competitions. It was sad to me because Wrexham AFC, the inaugural winners of the Welsh Cup in 1877/8 and winners of the cup a record 23 times, were barred from a competition to which they had contributed so much.

The Football Association of Wales should be given credit for their attempts to redeem this injustice with the introduction of the FAW Premier Cup. One of the few bright ideas to have come from the FAW, mind you. Last season's final (in the Invitation Cup as it was then) between Wrexham and Cardiff City was a great credit to Wales.

Knowing that the 1994/95 season would, for the time being at least, be Wrexham's last chance to play in Europe, I was particularly determined that the Webbed Robin would have a personal representation in Europe.

Wrexham won the 1994/95 Welsh Cup by defeating, yet again, Cardiff City at the Cardiff Arms Park. Due to Wales's lowly world ranking at the time, Wrexham were forced to play in the preliminary round of the ECWC and drawn against Petrolul Ploiesti of Romania. The report of the away leg remains the Webbed Robin's only excursion outside the United Kingdom. I won't bore you with the match details, we lost 0-1 following a goal-less first leg, but here's part of the story of the trip that I posted on the Webbed Robin.

"The day of the match was nice and sunny until we bought a newspaper that told us that the kick-off was at 5pm and not at 7pm as we were told back home. At the railway station in Bucharest we had to queue for an hour to get the train ticket (wrong queue initially but nothing to indicate otherwise) and caught the train as it was moving out of the station.

"Eventually we arrived in Ploiesti and caught a taxi to the ground. On the way there a policeman stopped the taxi at a crossroads and as the driver drove away he managed to knock down two pedestrians.

They were not badly injured but more than a little annoyed! Luckily the scene of the accident was within walking distance of the ground and so we walked the rest of the journey.

"After the game, as we were walking out, the Petrolul supporters gathered around us and showed great interest in our shirts. No one in Ploiesti wore the genuine Petrolul shirts since they are too expensive and they seemed to be very curious about the material that our shirts were made of. Offers of swaps with T-shirts were politely turned down.

"We had a beer at the main town square and talked with some Petrolul supporters who gave us postal stamps as a gift. On the train back we conversed with more supporters in the language of football – they all agreed that Karl Connolly was a very good player and should be playing for Manchester United! On the train we were given bunches of grapes as presents.

"And that was the end of a day full of mixed emotions. Our final day in Bucharest was spent sightseeing and that did not take us long. The city is not pretty at all (it makes Wrexham look like Vienna)."

Everybody has secrets but I'm not sure whether I'm wise to disclose to the nation the biggest skeleton in my cupboard. Anyway, here goes and I'll await the repercussions. The truth is that I was once a member of, ahem, Cardiff City Supporters' Club. Before any of my fellow Wrexham supporters start calling me a traitor, although I can empathise with them, there is, arguably, a perfectly valid reason for this aberration.

I spent three years as a poor student at Bristol University. During that period I tried to squeeze in as many Wrexham games as possible and squeeze was the operative term, both in terms of the Club's and my own financial situation. Although there is no way I'd classify myself as a fair-weather Wrexham supporter, I would admit to being quite selective as to which national football matches I go to see.

In 1991 the Welsh national side were doing very well thank you, in particular in the European Championship qualifiers. Their most notable success was a 1-0 victory at the now defunct Cardiff Arms Park (RIP) against World Champions Germany. The victory came courtesy of a Wrexham player (at least he is at the time of writing this piece) – one of Wales's greatest footballing legends, Ian Rush. On that great night, having witnessed scenes of pure joy and national pride, my brother and I decided over a few pints at the Old Arcade, Cardiff that we were going to go for the return match to be played somewhere in Germany. To be absolutely correct here, Wales had not just beaten the World Champions, they had done better than that – they'd just beaten the World Champions with East Germany tagged on.

So plans were afoot to make the trip to Nuremburg where the return leg was to be played at the brand new Frankenstadion. Problem is, we were skint. That was until my brother, who worked in Cwmbran, heard of a smashing deal (another operative word there!) whereby for 50-odd quid one would get a return coach journey from Newport to Nuremberg combined with a night's stay at a luxury hotel in Wumberg. Brilliant, I thought and handed the money over to my brother who booked us on the trip. It was only later that I found out that the trip was organised by the CCFC Supporters' Club and that a prerequisite of travelling was membership of the club. Caught between the devil and the deep blue sea I opted to spend 36 hours stuck in a bus with a bunch of Bluebirds. And with me masquerading as one of them!

That was an experience I will never forget or repeat. Needless to say, I kept my allegiance to the Mighty Robins to myself throughout the journey – too many visits to Ninian Park in the past had been less than comfortable. The trip was certainly an education. As we boarded the bus I was amused to see that attention to detail had not been missed. Down the whole corridor of the vehicle, hanging by shoelaces from the ceiling, were bottle openers. They came in very useful.

I was also amused by the organisers' choice of the on-board video to entertain the troops during the long journey. Just the one video – nothing dirty, nothing violent, not even X-rated. It was a video of Liverpool's 8-0 FA Cup drubbing of Swansea City the previous season! I swear to you that the cheers for the Liverpool goals were as if they were scoring for Cardiff – even on the twentieth showing as we passed through Brussels.

I won't delve into the less funny aspects of the trip, suffice to say that every club has its small share of nutters and Cardiff City FC are known not to be an exception. I just wish they hadn't been on my bloody bus.

The game? Well, we got thumped 1-4 with Wales scoring from the spot, the Euro '92 dream was gone. The match marked the introduction of a young winger winning his first cap for Wales. More than seven years on, Ryan Giggs should be challenging the likes of Rushie for the mantle of Wales's greatest. He is not.

It is both a pro and a con of running a football web site that one receives a significantly higher than average share of e-mails. It is very gratifying to receive e-mails from Wrexham and other clubs' supporters from all over the world who appreciate the services supplied by the Webbed Robin. The minority that criticise constructively are also welcome; without direction it would be harder to recognise required areas of improvement.

One of the most appreciated rewards of running The Webbed Robin was receiving acknowledgement from Peter Ward, the fulcrum of the Wrexham midfield. Peter's brother-in-law runs the Sunderland FC web site and e-mailed me to say that he was related to one of our players. At the time I was in hospital, having received surgery on a dodgy leg. Karen replied, informing him of my situation. By the end of the week a "Get Well Soon" card signed by all the players arrived at my bedside. It had been organised by Wardy himself. Peter is one of Wrexham's best players but even if he weren't he'd still be my favourite – a classy gesture from a classy player.

I suppose that I ought to expect a few followers of our closest rivals to e-mail me, mostly jovial banter but some more sinister. I'm not a vindictive person, not generally anyway. On a few occasions I have received some vile e-mails, some of which, amazingly, come from the workplace. A quick reply reminding the sender of the consequence of reporting their actions to their employers usually results in an immediate apology! I particularly enjoy the grovelling apologies when Chester fans send them. There are some right sickos out there.

With the Internet becoming more popular the traffic into the Webbed Robin is bound to increase. Time alone will tell how the web site will develop with this increase. Maybe the club itself will bring out an official web site so informative as to make the current content in the Webbed Robin redundant. If this were the case then I hope that the Webbed Robin is flexible enough to search into new avenues to keep the audience dialling in as they are currently do.

Granted, not spending 20 hours a week travelling to, watching and writing about football would give me a lot more free time but, as Janice Joplin said, "Freedom's just another word for nothing left to lose."

Twenty-Two Foreigners in Funny Shorts. The Intelligent Fan's Guide to Soccer and World Cup '94, Pete Davies, Random House, NY. ISBN 0-679-77493-9

Cardiff City On Line

Michael Morris – http://www.cardiffcity.co.uk

My first experiences of the Internet were in 1996. My first job was to find any Cardiff City information on the World Wide Web (www). After a lot of searching I could find only two or three poor web sites. Granted personal web site design was still in its infancy, but the effects were only half-hearted and rarely updated. As I was new to the www I did not even contemplate my own web site. Instead I tried to find other City fans on the net. Late in 1996 I came across Huw Thomas, a 1927 club member (Cardiff City Supporters in London). Huw had already established a link with about ten other City fans on the net. They would keep in contact by sending each other e-mails about twice a week.

After I became involved we managed to increase the group to around twenty people. Then we discovered a proper mailing list (ISFA) where you can send e-mails to a specific address and they are forwarded to everyone who has subscribed. Initially, weekly mails would total maybe twenty to thirty. The list has grown so rapidly that now you can receive up to 100 e-mails a day. Many are on various Cardiff City topics, many others bear no relevance to the football club but give serious comment on all manner of issues. There are some very funny mails too. The list seems to regulate itself. The subscribers have many thoughtful things to say, and if we get someone looking for trouble on the list they are quickly forced out.

It was early in 1997 that, as the list started to grow and I found myself more able to understand the Internet and how it worked, I decided to start my own web site. I did not want to be controversial, and in hindsight that was the best decision I made. I wanted to put out up-to-date information on Cardiff City and keep all the people who visited the site updated. My objective was to improve on the then current Cardiff web sites.

As soon as I get up-to-date information I put it on the site. It's no good having dated information as people soon get bored reading the same old stuff. The web site started off with the basics – name and address of the club and the latest result, with comments on the game. As things progressed I added to the information. When I started I would get between twenty to fifty hits a week only. Of course, only people on the mailing list visited it. The City fans abroad were regular visitors.

As with everything, word got around. I advertised the site on Internet search engines so people searching on the words Cardiff City FC would find me. Word of mouth, friends telling friends and the like also boosted visits to the site. After City lost in the semi-final of the 1997 play-offs we had a good readership.

As time went on the site began to get recognition throughout the Internet footballing world. It was linked from many other football sites and even recognised by the club itself, not officially but they knew we were there. I have to say the official Cardiff City web site at the time was a very poor show indeed. The updates were poor – if they were done at all. Now the feedback I get from supporters is the main reason I keep the site going. It's good to know that hundreds of City fans visit the site for information.

The 1998/99 season was massive. The list sponsored a player, Kevin Nugent; we gained promotion to Division Two; and I started to capture City goalscoring images for the visitors to my site to see. I have run competitions, we have a chat forum, and there is now total integration from the viewers. The web site today has over 80,000 requests for pictures a year and has 2,500 individual visitors a week.

The current City Chairman, Steve Borley, visits the chat forum, he answers questions directly from the fans. I don't think many other web sites can have this claim to fame except Gary Martin down the road. I know the City directors regularly visit the site, and I have been consulted by the club regards their own web site in recent times. In return, I put links from my site to various activities of the club such as the Centenary Club, credit cards and so on.

I have built up many friendships as a result of the web site, both in the club and throughout the world. The mailing list is a community within itself, with between fifteen and twenty members regularly meeting up before games. They also travel to games together.

At the end of last season, along with Leon Smith and Rebecca Greaves, I was privileged to make a presentation on the pitch at the promotion clincher against Scunthorpe United. This was to the groundsman for his sterling work. That presentation was on behalf of the list so it was a great honour. And all of this is with the backing of hundreds of Bluebirds worldwide.

The future? Well, next season the mailing list will continue to grow. We will be sponsoring two players at Ninian Park and will continue to support the club in its quest for the First Division. If you are looking for City information, check us out.

Chapter 5

The Media

For many years the vast majority of football fans outside of the capital city have believed that Cardiff has the monopoly on news stories and coverage. Wrexham say they have less than the South Wales clubs, Swansea less than Cardiff, the League of Wales less than everyone. Nevertheless, there are individuals who love the game and report on it passionately and, most of the time, fairly. Here are some of those individuals, representing the newspapers of West, South and North Wales and the nation. They, too, love the game and love to get their views across. We also have a passionate account from a BBC reporter in Cardiff and a view from one of the most familiar voices on Radio Wales.

Steve James is a Radio Wales reporter working for the BBC in Cardiff, he has worked on the sports desk for many years and now fronts many football-related shows throughout the season. We all know his voice. Steve is one of the many Newport County supporters who since the demise of their club have found a big gap in their lives. He has a passion for Welsh football, no matter the level and, more importantly, no matter the team. Here are some of Steve's personal reflections on the Welsh game.

My View of The Future

Steve James

To the world outside we are a rugby nation. There are, though, thousands upon thousands of us who play or watch football with as much passion for the beautiful game as any Brazilian. We don't want second-best soccer and we certainly don't deserve it. If this is the case, then why do we leave Wales by the busload every match day to witness the very best?

Will we always have to head for Anfield, Old Trafford, Highbury and Stamford Bridge to watch first-class soccer? Are we destined to be bystanders when other nations assemble to decide who is the best in Europe or the world? Some of you will say, "Yes". Others may disagree, but without much conviction. Some may not care at all.

Cardiff City fans have enjoyed a good 1999, Swansea have had many plus points too. There have even been moments for Wrexham fans to shout about. In the main, however, their season was mediocre. Barry Town fans have had the success they expected and are used to. Newport AFC have been celebrating. Supporters at Aberystwyth, Cwmbran, Caernarfon, Inter CableTel, Newtown and many others have seen some entertaining football. The Welsh team managed some victories that few of us would have predicted.

New talent also emerged – the precious Craig Bellamy, for example. And we also had the rags to riches tale of Mark Delaney from Carmarthen to Aston Villa thanks to Frank Burrows and Billy Ayre. If you enjoyed the games, that's great. If you supported your team on the good days and the bad days, brilliant. If your team gave you more to cheer than moan about, then fantastic. But don't you want more? Of course you do. Do players want to play in the big games, win trophies, hit the big time? Of course they do.

Most fans and players will always be ambitious. But what about those who run our game? A lack of ambition seems to be a constant in Welsh soccer. There have been too many people at the helm of our clubs who don't care or can't make it happen, too many chairmen with hidden agendas? And there are people in charge of the game in Wales who lose track of the real goal. They put themselves and their ambitions before the good of the game. There are those, of course, who just make a downright mess of things too.

So what can we do? Put up with what we get, go elsewhere for our football fix? **No.** It's up to everyone of us to do our bit. Tell your boss to invest in football. Don't just go and watch the game, give something back. Get involved, get on committees and encourage kids to play the game. Support the people who are doing their best to improve the game in Wales. Take friends to games, help combat the mindless thugs who tarnish our game, respect your fellow fans and those who support a different team. Share their love of the game.

Of course we enjoyed last season. We love football. We would, of course, like to enjoy next season too. Wales is not the hotbed of football, but the dragon breathes fire. It's up to you to keep the flame alive.

Grahame Lloyd is a freelance broadcaster and journalist based in Cardiff. Once HTV football commentator, he writes on the game for Rothmans Football Yearbook. He is also the author of Daffodil Days: Glamorgan's Glorious Summer (Gomer), the official celebration of the 1997 county championship win; Jan the Man: From Anfield to Vetch Field (Victor Gollancz), the life story of Jan Molby, the former Swansea City player manager; and C'mon City! A Hundred Years of the Blue-birds (Seren), the official celebration book for Cardiff City's centenary. His contribution here is characteristically entertaining and thought-provoking.

Funny Old Game, Football

Grahame Lloyd

One minute Bobby Gould was in charge of the Welsh team; the next he was co-presenting a daytime phone-in programme on national radio. And in between, he had reached the short-list for the vacant manager's job at Sheffield United.

Not content with Andy Warhol's fifteen minutes of fame, Gould spent three hours helping to chair debates on the European elections, the Shadow Cabinet reshuffle and the Glastonbury Festival. The invitation was the result of an attempt to compare the different pressure levels of live radio presentation and international football management.

No matter how successful his performance in the Radio 5 Live studio, the Bramall Lane interview ended in failure – as did Gould's four-year spell in charge of Wales. For the record, Wales lost 13 of his 24 games, winning just seven and drawing four. They're no nearer reaching the finals of a major tournament for the first time for 40 years – despite back-to-back wins over Denmark and Belarus in autumn 1998. Some critics even claim that Welsh football has taken at least one step backwards under Gould. To be fair to him, he couldn't stand the heat so he left the kitchen.

When he replaced Mike Smith in 1994, Gould promised to put a smile back on the face of Welsh football; the trouble was that in doing so he became a figure of fun – a role he appeared to relish. Wearing his heart on his sleeve, the former Coventry and Wimbledon manager let it rule his head in his dealings with players and the press. He once appeared at a news conference wearing a Max Wall mask and his reign was littered with bust-ups with players, most famously his reprimand of Robbie Savage for light-heartedly throwing away an Italian shirt in a television interview.

Then there was a very public slanging match with one of his predecessors, John Toshack, not to mention a series of horrendous defeats including 6-4 to Turkey, 7-1 to Holland and 4-0 to Italy which sent him on his way. Having quickly negotiated the settlement of his contract, Gould explained that he had resigned in "the best interests of Welsh football."

It's hard to disagree with his assessment. Almost single-handedly, Gould had united a nation by quitting. With little success, respect from his players or tactical nous, he really had no alternative. The search for his successor, like Bobby Gould himself, is an open book.

Away from the field, the FAW hardly covered themselves in glory during the 1998-99 season through their obsession with making money. The fall-out from the "cash-for-votes" scandal led to Keith Wiseman and Graham Kelly falling on their swords at Lancaster Gate. The FAW's secretary-general David Collins didn't even bother looking for his scabbard. He and the 20 or so councillors emerged from the whole grubby affair with their positions intact but their reputations in tatters.

The Welsh FA also caught a cold after a pitifully low crowd turned up to see Denmark win 2-0 at Anfield. The game was crying out to be played at Ninian Park in Cardiff but the deal had been done and UEFA rejected a last-minute appeal to switch the venue. So no big bucks or Euro 2000 points either.

At club level, Welsh football looks far healthier. Cardiff City are back in Division Two at the start of their centenary season with a board of local businessmen rather than one apparently wealthy individual in charge. If they can match manager Frank Burrows in terms of ambition, then Division One might be a realistic target in the near future.

Swansea City flattered to deceive by reaching the Third Division play-offs after one of their most inconsistent seasons to date. With no money to improve his squad, manager John Hollins worked a minor miracle at the Vetch Field but the purse strings need to be loosened if the Swans are to begin their new life at the Morfa Stadium in a new division.

Sadly, the long-overdue development of the Racecourse coincided with Wrexham's unexpected decline. They struggled for much of the season and Man Flynn's rebuilding programme is well underway. Let's hope they soon have a better team – and support – to match their improved ground.

In the League of Wales, congratulations must go once again to Barry Town (champions for the umpteenth time and the winners of the Gilbert League Cup and the FAW Premier Cup) and to Inter CableTel, now Cardiff, who finished second in the championship and also qualified for Europe by winning the Welsh Cup.

As the new millennium beckons, one of the unexplained mysteries of the twentieth century needs to be addressed. With attendances and viewing figures continuing to show that football is the most popular game in the world, why hasn't the League of Wales attracted a sponsor?

Jonathon Wilshire is a South Wales Evening Post journalist. Jon writes on a daily basis about his local team, Swansea City. Brought up supporting the Swans as a child he now has the enviable job of commenting on the side and its many transformations for a living. Jon, though, sees it differently. He does love his job, but maybe this insight into how he compiles his work after a game would put a few off.

Watching Football is the Best Job in the World

Jonathon Wilshire

Many a football fan has accused those of us treading the career path of sports journalism of enjoying the best job in the world. Watching two teams kick the hell out of a bit of leather and writing about it afterwards – nothing could be easier or more enjoyable. Watching football and getting paid for it must be the best job in the world. I even thought that once.

Now don't get me wrong, I enjoy football with the best of them. I was brought up kicking a can as a kid and standing on the old metal girders at the back of the North Bank as the Swans rattled through the divisions. Football, as for every true fan, is in the blood. Not just at football league level, but also local league, Welsh League and The League of Wales. I've covered them all in my time and even played a bit. I still do cover them all.

Having spent ten years in the job (where the duties also include page design), I don't suppose it's surprising when I say the novelty has waned a bit. Travelling to the likes of Hartlepool, Carlisle, Hull and Darlington on a wet and cold winter's day is hardly the stuff to set the pulses racing. Watching the Third Division these days tends to have the same effect.

Luckily, one of the perks of the job is that you don't have to pay to watch the games. I don't know if I would splash out ten pounds to stand on the terraces these days. I would probably take in a Welsh League game instead. For that reason it often makes my blood boil to see the fans paying at the turnstile, far more dedicated supporters than me, being taken for granted by football clubs. Football, clubs keep telling us, is an entertainment industry, unfortunately most of them only put on a pantomime on a Saturday afternoon, and often there is no matinee.

Most Third Division grounds are antiquated. The facilities on offer to the cash-paying public are usually worse. The fans, though, can sleep soundly in the knowledge that facilities for the press, those who always see a different game to those on the terraces, are just as bad. Take the Vetch press box, for example, a press box that once housed every national newspaper on a regular basis as John Toshack's Swansea City rose and topped the old First Division. That press box, situated on the top of the centre stand and looking a fairly substantial affair to those on the North Bank, tells only half the story these days. It's spilt in two now, with the police enjoying the half closest to the centre circle, the best view of the game. And the innocent fan? It's quite comical watching the visiting journalists scampering up the old rickety steps to the box on match days. They end up with a restricted view and a seat in the stalls.

The wooden plank that acts as a bench has now been sanded down and painted glossy black to prevent any cheeky splinters, but while those paid to report on the game may sit comfortably, they can't see the pitch! It's even a strain for those in the front row of the press box for big black boards separating the windows and restricting the view are positioned every few seats along. Establishing the corner taker and throw-in taker at the far end of the centre stand involves a quick window opening exercise and leaning out. Sadly, the Swansea press box rates with the worst of them. That's the scenario at most Third Division grounds these days.

Rotherham's box is equally unimpressive. Its press box must have been designed with the sole purpose of doubling up as a pigeon loft during the close season. But at Rotherham you do get a free pie from the friendly pie man at half-time.

The Third Division really is a different world. The local Swansea hacks were even rubbing their hands in anticipation of moving up to the glitz of the Second Division this season. The grounds of the likes of Reading, Man City, Millwall, Bristol Rovers and Bristol City were spoken of as mini-Wembleys, unfortunately, the play-offs ended those dreams and it's now back to Carlisle, Hartlepool, Darlington and Hull.

It was whilst on a spying mission to Derby, Swansea's fourth-round FA Cup opponents, that my eyes were really opened to how the other half lives. Greeted and treated like royalty by Rams employees dressed in the top gear, no request was too much trouble. A huge buffet was set out in a large press room, and you wondered where the hidden agenda was. But this, I was told by the local hack, was uniform throughout the Premiership. So that's what I've been missing.

Watching the game itself, however, is the easy bit. The spoken word these days is almost as important, if not more so, as what happens on the pitch. Looking back through the old *Evening Post* cuttings of twenty years ago, a match report was just that, a match report. There were very few quotations, just the facts of the game in great detail. These days the views of the manager or the hero of the hour form the basis of the report. The major match details are worked in neatly around those views, and often as an afterthought.

Apart from the match report, there are even more views from the manager, chairman, players and even fans dominating the back page. Add another two or three stories as an off-shoot to the major fare and there are usually enough words to fill a book let alone a newspaper. And like most things these days the pressures have got greater; more work and less time to do it.

Take Swansea's play-off semi-final trip to Scunthorpe as an example. This is the diary of the local hack. Of course, this is after you have persuaded the powers that be that an overnight stay is required. After all, I had an eight-hour round trip to fit in as well as a game, match report and, indeed, two hour's sleep. As usual, a book was requested for the second leg.

1pm: Set off on the long drive from Swansea

5pm: Book in at B&B

7.45pm: Kick-off

9.30pm: End of normal time with the scores level on aggregate

9.45pm: Extra time

10.20pm: Swansea's Wembley dream ends in tears

10.30pm: No press conference organised as usual. I join the rest of the journalists scraping for quotes outside the dressing room

11.30pm: Interviews in the can with John Hollins, Brian Laws, Steve Hamer, Mathew Bound, Nick Cusack, Roger Freestone, Gareth Sheldon, and Uncle Tom Cobley

11.55pm: Back at the B&B

1.30am: Finished transcribing notes from tape recorder

4am: Finished match report and two "quotes" pieces

6am: Wake to finished writing the story for the back page

8am: Call office to ensure they have received the stories from my laptop

9am: Breakfast

10am: Start the four-hour journey back to Swansea

2pm: Arrive back in the office. Start work on the following day's back-page story with Mathew Bound. All on two hours' sleep!

You can probably now understand why I enjoy leaving the notebook behind now and again and becoming just another spectator. It gives me a chance to watch from the sidelines and even show the odd emotion without Mr Neutral looking on in disgust.

One of these memorable trips came back in 1997, the year Swansea made it to Wembley again. For the semi-final we went to Chester's Legoland ground in the first leg.

Having scrounged a seat on Trevor Bond's barmy army minibus from The Royal Exchange in Briton Ferry, we wound our way through 'B' class roads to Chester. As we trundled through Chester, passing the historic walls, we were met by a house brick perfectly wrapped inside a sacrificial scarf. Luckily for me it was my seated companion who felt the full force of the splintered glass as it shattered one of the side windows. He got a gashed eye. I got a neat splatter of his blood forming a designer pattern down the front of my jeans. It made scrounging a press pass for the game that much harder when we eventually crawled in to Legoland's car park. But worse was yet to come – from the heavens.

A four-hour bus journey home is bad enough. When you have drawn the short straw to sit next to the broken window, just as the heavens have opened up, you know that your luck has run out. Sitting shivering for four hours, a black bin liner taking the role of a raincoat, made the office car and my trusty notebook seem very appealing. Swansea slaughtered Chester in the second leg and the fans were so loud the Chester fans must have felt more uncomfortable than I had after the first leg. It was one of those times when even I think I have the best job in the world!

Dave Lovett is Wrexham-born and bred. He writes for the Wrexham Evening Leader and has done so for many years. The piece that follows is not only from a working journalist, however – Dave is also a passionate supporter of Wrexham AFC. The European adventure for Welsh clubs has always been forwarded by Wrexham. With the exception of Cardiff City's Real Madrid adventure, Wrexham certainly have the most to shout about. Dave's piece also indicates that they have very high hopes for the year 2000 and beyond.

The Millennium with High Hopes

Dave Lovett

The new stand at The Racecourse. Proof that rebuilding can be done in Wales.

There is already a futuristic look about the Racecourse, where a redevelopment costing three and a half million pounds will be ready for next season. Wrexham fans are going up the wall about it, quite literally. A name-a-brick scheme has attracted attention from all over the world. But the real name of the game remains team building as Wrexham again reach out for the First Division. The mortar crumbled inexplicably last season. Wrexham were one of the pre-season top tips for promotion and the arrival of Wales and Liverpool legend Ian Rush only reinforced the optimism. But somehow it all went pear-shaped for Wrexham and Ian Rush, and they escaped relegation by just three points.

The sad fact is that Ian Rush did not score in 27 league and cup games, and for him that has to be some record. Also, Wrexham conceded too many goals. There was an acrimonious glove story between goalkeeper Andy Marriot and manager Brian Flynn. That ended with the fans' favourite Marriot moving to Sunderland, and yes, after only two months of the campaign. Flynn turned to the number two, Mark Cartwright. Before the season was out Northern Ireland International Tommy Wright replaced him. He was, of course, only on loan from Manchester City. He couldn't do right for doing wrong and before the season ended he was on the transfer list. Rookie David Walsh came in for the £100,000 showpiece FA Premier Cup final clash with Barry Town. Wrexham embarrassingly lost the game.

Flynn has since signed a new keeper, Kevin Dearden from Brentford, and he will be the key component this time as Wrexham strive to regain past glories.

Giant Killers

Wrexham have chopped down a few beanstalks in their time, at home and abroad. Over the years the FA Cup has been a happy hunting ground and there are quite a few scalps hanging from their totem pole. Managers John Neal, Arfon Griffiths and Flynn have all taken Wrexham to FA Cup quarter-finals over the past two decades. All three also took them into Europe via the Welsh Cup.

Neal was the avuncular Geordie who wouldn't say boo to a goose. Under his shrewd management, however, Wrexham ruffled quite a few feathers. It was Neal who took Wrexham into Europe for the first time in 1972. Albert Kinsey scored their first European goal in a 1-1 draw in Zurich. Goals by Mel Sutton and Billy Ashcroft made the Swiss roll during the home leg.

Four years later Wrexham were back in Europe again with Neal still in charge. They beat teams from Sweden and Poland before gallantly losing over two legs to the eventual winners, Anderlecht. Neal's Wrexham also came astonishingly close to promotion from the old Third Division before he moved on to Middlesborough.

Arfon Griffiths, his right-hand man took over affairs in May 1977. Under his management his home town-club won the Third Division championship. Bill Shankley described that Wrexham side as the best Third Division side he had ever seen. It included good pros like goalkeeper Dai Davies and defenders John Roberts and Gareth

Davies. Then there were gifted players like Mickey Thomas, Bobby Shinton, Graham Whittle and deadeye Dixie McNeil. They trounced Rotherham before an ecstatic Racecourse crowd on April 22nd 1978 to clinch promotion. It was a wonderful, never-to-be-forgotten day. "Arfon's Army" also marched into Europe. They went to Yugoslavia and played Rijeka in a stadium spectacularly hewn out of a cliff overlooking the Adriatic.

The following year the Wrexham trailblazers defeated FC Magdeburg, 3-2 at The Racecourse but lost a dramatic second leg in East Germany in extra time. Nothing, of course, lasts forever and Griffiths steadfastly refused to compromise his principles to appease directors, and left.

Wrexham's next expedition into Europe was in 1984/85, by which time Scot Bobby Roberts was manager. He had a difficult time at then cash-strapped Wrexham, but what a time they had in Europe. Wrexham went into the European Cup Winners Cup

Wrexham FC: The first winners of the Welsh Cup in 1888. They hold the record of 23 cup final victories.

draw and, Jack Horner-style, pulled the plum FC Porto. Big Jim Steele, now a Merseyside copper, scored the goal that beat the Portuguese side in the first leg. But no one gave Roberts' ragtag-and-bobtail outfit an earthly chance in Oporto. It rained cats and dogs that night and Fourth Division Wrexham were soon 3-0 down. Defender Jake King crowned a memorable night by scoring twice and Barry Horne made it 4-3. That made it 4-4 on aggregate. I couldn't believe it; Wrexham had gone through on the away goals' rule.

Roberts was dragged fully clothed into the showers that night as Wrexham celebrated. They flew home in a thunderstorm. Their reward was a tie against AS Roma. They went to the Eternal City to enjoy themselves, and they did. Goalkeeper Stuart Parker played the game of his life in the Olympic Stadium as Wrexham lost 2-0. Roma won 1-0 at Wrexham.

Roberts' reign ended in 1985 and Wrexham then turned to hero Dixie McNeil. He also took the club to Europe. They won in Malta before losing out in extra time to Real Zaragoza. McNeil, like Roberts, found it impossible to manage because of a lack of cash, he quit in October 1989. Flynn took over and is now the club's longest serving manager. He, too, has tasted European football as manager. Wrexham beat Danish side Lyngby before going out to Manchester United. His turning point came on an overcast January afternoon in 1992.

Arsenal, League champions, arrived in North Wales for a third-round FA Cup tie. The Gunners took the lead through Alan Smith and everyone sat back to await the cricket score result. Enter Thomas. He scored a fabulous free-kick to draw the teams then Steve Watkin scored the winner, the name of Wrexham reverberated around Europe. One Wrexham fan in Hong Kong saw the result on the TV. He immediately hailed a rickshaw and went out and had a ball. Commemorative T-shirts were produced to mark the victory. Many were sold to the fans of the other North London team – Tottenham Hotspur.

Wrexham fans have long had a genuine concern for their stadium. At last the blinkers are off and redevelopment is forthcoming. The centrepiece will be a new 3,500 all-seater stand to be named after Chairman Pryce Griffiths. Paddocks below the other two stands have been seated. Griffiths is proud of the rebuilding which restores

Ian Rush: now departed from The Racecourse. His most surprising statistic: no league goals for Wrexham.

Wrexham as an international stadium for both football and rugby. Wales no longer have to travel to controversial venues like Anfield to play home fixtures. Rugby fans will see the World Cup at The Racecourse.

Pryce Griffiths is a lifelong Wrexham fan who can truly claim to have made it from terrace to boardroom. He once wheelbarrowed concrete to help build The Racecourse Kop. "That was a long time ago," he said, "but our future here at Wrexham is now looking rosier than it has for some time. The new ground improvements and our 125-year lease give us security. All we want now is promotion to the First Division." Amen.

Chapter 6

A Welshman at the World Cup

Martin Johnes

Martin Johnes lives and works in Cardiff. In search of the ultimate footballing experience he went to the 1998 World Cup. He still dreams of success for Wales in the competition!

Giggs skips past Roberto Carlos and chips in a beautiful cross. Harston jumps... Oohh! What a header! Taffarel is left motionless as the ball hits the back of the net. It's Wales one, Brazil nil in this World Cup Group A match.

Okay, you can stop dreaming. Wales didn't make it to the World Cup finals. Again. But there's always 2002. I quite fancy a holiday in Japan and South Korea. Then again, the World Cup is meant to be a global celebration of football and there's no reason why that should be limited to people lucky enough to live in countries with decent sides or lucky draws.

So with my Wales shirt packed into my rucksack, off I headed to France. My team may not have been going but I wasn't going to miss out. Montpellier looked a nice town from travel books and, with Paraguay playing Bulgaria there, there had to be a reasonable chance of picking up tickets without paying out my three months' wages.

Montpellier is a strange city. A beautiful centre comprised of grand old buildings arranged around an impressive square complete with statues and fountains. Beyond that is a mix of dark and narrow streets hiding cafés, shops and endless dog excrement and graffiti. Beyond that is the Mediterranean and a host of shack-like buildings crumbling in the sun. However, for now the city was given over to the most spectacular event in the world (as the huge signs reminded us): the World Cup. Endless flags and signs, fifty-foot photographs hanging from buildings, a giant screen showing all the matches and table football games hiding down alleys made sure that no one could forget just what was going on.

Gradually, the fans began to arrive. During my brief stay, Paraguay, Bulgaria, Morocco and Norway all played in Montpellier. The Norwegians wore their Viking helmets, the Moroccans ran around making as much noise as possible, the Paraguayans wore every colour imaginable and the Bulgarians, well, they just chanted a lot.

Apart from the followers of the teams playing in the city, there were Dutch in orange wigs, Scots in kilts, drunken Englishmen behaving themselves, Brazilians in anything and everything yellow, and even a few Frenchmen. In such a kaleidoscope of colour my Wales shirt did not exactly stand out but it did draw the attention of every football fan that walked past. Cue confusion.

I got mistaken for being from Morocco, Norway, Spain, Bordeaux (something to do with the colour of their away strip) and, of course, once they heard what language I spoke, England. Trying to explain the difference between Wales and England in schoolboy French to someone whose English isn't much better is nigh on impossible. The odd rugby fan got it straight away but, despite our membership of the world of football nations and my desperate word association, most people took a while to understand.

"Pays de Galles?! Either my pronunciation is terrible or our fame has really not spread across the channel. Or maybe both.

"Ryan Giggs?" Blank look or a reply of Manchester United but no recognition that he was Welsh.

"Ian Rush?" Another blank look.

"Diana!" This usually worked, but it seems pretty sad that our nation has been reduced to being identified by a dead English royal (albeit a very nice one before I get shouted at).

If this didn't work I either just gave up or just said I was Scottish. The tartan presence at the World Cup at least made this recognisable and after their performance against Brazil claiming to be a Scot usually went down well.

Luckily, the day English fans in Marseilles decided to demonstrate their 'hardness' by wrecking cafés and shouting at passers-by was the day I left France. Being mistaken for being English is one thing but such confusion after a bunch of thugs had decided to make England

Wales at The World Cup? Bridges burned, chances had, thanks to Scotland.

the most hated country in Europe is quite another. Nonetheless, in one French café the reputation of the English had preceded the fans and a bloke at the bar gave me a long lecture on how great Ireland, Scotland and Wales are, followed by a rant on how arrogant and stupid the English are. Or at least I think that's what he said.

So my Wales shirt was a great way of meeting people, but at the same time being Welsh made me feel a bit left out. Despite the French hospitality, the excitement in the square with the big screen, and the general party atmosphere, there were times when I felt not quite part of it. Dancing in fountains, waving flags at everyone in the street and singing endless tuneless songs was fine for those people whose teams had qualified but I would have felt a fraud fully joining in. No quantity of red wine let me forget that Giggs, Hughes and Co. were at home. The party was great but I could never quite lose that feeling I'd gatecrashed somewhere I should not be.

Acquiring tickets for Paraguay-Bulgaria proved cheap and easy but I was a bit disappointed to have to sit behind a couple from Newcastle and in front of a group of blokes in Aston Villa tops. England was obviously destined to haunt me on this trip. And then to add to

trip's painful reminder that I came from a country that had not qualified for a major tournament for 40 years was the grandeur of the stadium. It ensured I remembered that once the summer was over I had
to go back to supporting a mediocre team playing in a Third Division
shack.

Oh well, you can't choose either your club or country (not without
selling out or glory hunting anyway), and it will different in 2002.
We'll qualify next time, I know it. 'Bread of Heaven' in a Tokyo foun-
tain anyone? We can always dream

Chapter 7

Playing Away from Home

David Collins

I don't know how many people named Dave Collins you know, but while compiling this book I had three of them asking if they could put some "ooomph" into the follow-up to Come on Cymru! Contributions from two of them appear in the next two chapters.

The first is the editor of Welsh Football magazine and based in Cardiff. In the magazine he and his regular contributors cover many aspects of the game in Wales and the number of subscribers increases monthly. The front cover illustrated in this book shows a West Wales game between Carew and Hakin. See Carew Castle in the background? Great stuff.

The other Dave Collins is a Cardiff City fan. He also lives in the capital and has supplied us with some impressive accounts of following Cardiff City and Wales. But more of him in the next chapter.

I am asked from time to time how someone born in London, with no Welsh connections, came to be such a passionate supporter and devotee of Welsh football; what drove me to devote so much time and effort to developing and sustaining Wales's national football magazine; and why, as a one-time supporter of one of Wales's 'exiles' playing in English non-league football, I believe so firmly that clubs based in Wales should be playing in its national competitions, and not in an alien system. Indeed, from time to time I even ask myself these questions. I can only really try to answer them by telling the story of my own lifelong love affair with football and the events that have led me here.

Before I start that story, though, I must clear up one detail: although my name is David Collins, I am not, definitely NOT the Secretary General of the Football Association of Wales! The fact that I share my name with the holder of that office is a constant source of confu-

Carew v. Hakin. A cover from Welsh Football *magazine.*

sion and must have been an inconvenience to both of us in recent years. So now you can read on, safe in the knowledge that you're not going to encounter 'official' FAW views in this article.

I fell in love with football at first sight. Nine years old, with no previous interest in the sport, I was taken to Plough Lane, home of Wimbledon in the Southern League. I can still remember that first match, Wimbledon v Sittingbourne, September 1964, and how I felt on discovering this new dimension to life. Somehow I knew then that Wimbledon would always be my club, an enduring love, and so it has been and will be. Not that there haven't been others, as we shall see, I've played the field, tried to get involved at times, but it's no good, and I've accepted that now. And knowing that has certainly made it so much easier to be a generally impartial observer of Welsh club soccer.

But I also think that, even from those very early days in SW19, besides a devotion to my club, there was more to my interest: a fascination with the diversity of the clubs that came to play the Dons, with the places they came from and a curiosity about their grounds in (seemingly) faraway places. Amongst the most distant, and therefore exciting, of the visitors were the Welsh clubs, Barry Town and Merthyr Tydfil, sadly both a long way out of the range of away trips I was allowed. Indeed, I remember reading that the Dons team had even been flown to their away game at Barry! In addition to the Welsh clubs, there was John Charles, who came first with Hereford and later with Merthyr and who, of all the players I saw in the Southern League, probably made the most vivid impression. Though well past his prime, the power and stature of the man were unmistakable and unforgettable.

Otherwise, my knowledge of Wales in my London youth was pretty limited, mainly consisting no doubt of the (generally unflattering) images on television: Aberfan, miners' strikes, rugby, "How Green Was My Valley" on the television.... Non-league football didn't get much press coverage in those days and for a Londoner, even one with a developing interest in the remote and obscure, Welsh football was a closed book. I had no awareness of a Welsh League, north or south, and probably knew the names of more Maltese, Luxembourgeoise and Icelandic clubs than Welsh ones through their appearance in the UEFA competitions. I was already fascinated by the fact that clubs from these smaller nations could represent them in international competition. But at that time it didn't occur to me that Wales was under-represented; like most Englishmen (and perhaps many a Welshman to this day?) I'd always assumed Wales was more or less part of England. After all, Scotland had its own league on the football pools, but Welsh clubs all played in the English leagues! I am sure I was far from alone.

By 1980 work brought me to live in Cardiff and for quite a long time it didn't cross my mind to be anything other than an exiled Wimbledon supporter, watching my team only very occasionally. With a young family and growing work commitments, I wasn't looking for another call on my time and energies anyway. After a few years I began to feel something was missing, that football had been relegated to a role too insignificant in my life. Now feeling settled and established in Wales, I wondered if there might be enjoyment to be found in football close to home. Somehow this idea of a football supporter's equivalent of a 'bit on the side' no longer seemed as unfaithful a thought as it would once have done, especially since the Dons were doing well enough without me and had now risen well beyond their non-league roots. But where to start? I'd been devoted to one club for so long that I'd almost forgotten how to meet new clubs.

I ventured to Ninian Park but found nothing appealing there: an air of decline and despair prevailed most of the time, when City were under-achieving. Whenever things started to improve, an even worse climate of hostility emerged. I would never have any affection for Cardiff City. I tried Barry Town, a familiar old name from my Southern League days, but – despite the Linnets' strong Welsh League side – I came away from ramshackle old Jenner Park knowing I could not join the weekly referee-baiting ritual of the Town faithful of that time. (I hasten to add that the Barry fans today are a nicer bunch altogether!)

It was to be with Merthyr Tydfil that I had my first serious Welsh 'fling'. Something about Penydarren Park felt right and I knew I could grow fond of the Martyrs. For several years, fortunately an era when Lyn Jones's side was building to a peak of scintillating football with the likes of Paul Giles, Dave Webley and Ceri Williams, I counted Merthyr as very much 'my' team in Wales – not displacing Wimbledon in my affections, but definitely joining them. The flame lingers even today, though I abandoned Merthyr in despair when they chose to continue their inevitable decline in English non-league soccer and spurned the chance to dominate the new national league in the 1990s. It is painful, though, to see how low the club has sunk, while old rivals Barry Town and arrivistes like Inter Cardiff have seized the moment and exploited the opportunities opening up at home in Wales and in Europe,

However, I wasn't content with just following Merthyr in the late 1980s, for whilst exploring the footballing 'talent' on offer in South Wales I'd also got hooked on visiting new clubs and new grounds. I wasn't too liberal or promiscuous with my affections, for mostly these were just visits, mere one-match stands if you like. Every now and then, however, there was that extra chemistry and I'd get involved with another club for a while, as in the heady few weeks in 1990 when I supported the wonderfully named Ragged School as they surged through a series of giant-killings to win the Welsh Intermediate Cup.

I suppose it was through these travels across Wales, in search of new grounds and interesting fixtures, that I developed a feeling for Welsh football as distinct from football in England. The mood of the times was one of polarised debate over the pros and cons of the League of Wales and I found myself increasingly impatient with the lack of imagination and pride shown by so many true Welsh people. They ridiculed the idea of Wales being a footballing country with a league of its own, as if they felt somehow that their nation was less of one than every other UEFA country. Why is it only the Welsh have so little national pride that they want to play their football in another country's system? You don't find the top clubs in, say, Belgium, wanting to play in the German Bundesliga nor even those of Luxembourg seeing the Dutch or Belgian systems as the way forward. And so, through my incomprehension of the idea that clubs would rather soldier on in lowly leagues in another country, I became – rather incongruously given my roots – a fervent supporter of the League of Wales in its infancy. And have continued to support it ever since as it grows to fulfil its potential.

How I got so involved in *Welsh Football* magazine is harder to explain, though an unfulfilled journalistic alter ego is the main reason. Having gained so much pleasure myself from watching football all over Wales, from national league to parks grounds and from valley communities to the splendid scenic rural grounds, I enjoy being able to share that enjoyment through our magazine. And undoubtedly that's easier to do when you don't really support any particular Welsh club. But also, believing, as I have said, in Wales as a separate football nation and not "part of England", I want it to continue to have its own "flagship" publication.

And so today I often think of myself as being more Welsh than English. I have spent most of my adult life here and, though many fellow immigrants can't understand it, I cheer as loudly for Wales as anyone born here – and, yes, that would be the case if Wales played England, too. Like most football fans, my first club allegiance remains to the club of my youth (hence I was possibly the only Dons fan who thought the idea of a move to Cardiff not such a bad idea!). But 99% of my football life today is based here in Wales, and while Wimbledon have gone on to the heights of the Premiership, the football I watch most of the time is closer to the Southern League fare I grew up with, and I prefer it that way. It is, as a fellow countryman of mine once said, a funny old game.

Chapter 8

Cardiff City and Wales

David Collins

*Dave Collins is Cardiff City through and through but in "Oh, How We Danced" he remembers a night when he could have easily swapped spit with the most ardent Swansea City fan in the world. The place is the National Stadium as it was, the time is etched in the memory forever. This account is a particular favourite of mine. He continues with another international adventure – "Down in a Tube Station at Midnight" – which details a young man's journey from Cardiff to London in the late seventies as Wales took on and beat an England side that clearly underestimated the dragon's fire. Finally, he attempts to justify his passion for **his** team, something we all have to do at times, regardless of the team we follow. Dave Collins and fans like him are the reason why books such as this are needed. It gives a platform for his talent and his writing continues to feed the habit that is football. He has found his feet in this book. I hope you enjoy his style and passion for Welsh football as much as I have.*

Oh, How We Danced

It all started calmly enough. Seats had been booked well in advance for an all-ticket affair in the works' social (The City club would you believe?). Beers and a chat before the big one against the Germans. Thirty-eight thousand people were going to be in Cardiff for a football match, there was no way I was going to miss this one, no way at all, and I was going to enjoy every minute of it.

At four o' clock I was comfortably sat in The City club (80p a pint), cosily sipping in what I'd promised to be the first of only one or two gentle pre-match looseners. So, after five or six gentle looseners, the Arms Park beckoned – the call of the wild, Westgate Street, Cardiff, flags and scarves all around, hot dog vans, the lot. Could this be our night? Could this be the one?

Inside the ground the atmosphere was overpowering. The anthem boomed out. Hymns and arias demanded a Welsh victory. Behind us the biggest banner I have ever seen proclaimed "Cardiff City, Wales, Bluebirds" along three giant red and white stripes. There must have been twenty fellas holding it up.

Whenever I watch big matches on the TV I turn to my two-year-old boy and assure him, "One day it'll be our turn, son, and you watch us go." Tonight was our turn. It seemed the whole of Wales was there.

Amidst this ocean of passion, a football match was taking place far beneath us. Cagey and ever nervous, our side pitted themselves against the slick, confident and assured master race of world football.

Barry Horne hit the bar. The Germans stroked the ball about the racy Arms Park pitch. I was witnessing the masters at work: Brehme, Voller, Matthaus. It was inspiring but it was frightening. We had Ian Rush and Neville Southall. The last match I had attended had been Cardiff City v Maidstone. It seemed a thousand miles away.

The Germans moved freely, always a man in space. Mexican waves sprung up under the giant stands. A bad sign. The hwyl was dissolving. A guy in a Wrexham shirt urged more noise. I responded with The Ayatollah, but frenzied slaps on the head fell on deaf ears.

In the second half, as a thousand urine streams flowed into the waters of the Taff, Berthold booted Ratcliffe and a bright red card changed the course of history. The crowd exploded. We would never have a better chance and the team knew it. A previously tense Paul Bodin found Ian Rush in space and in front of goal. The keeper stayed put. A bulging net, and I was thrown into the air. Four of us fell over in a line along the back of the seats. I clawed my way to the gangway to stand rigid, scarf held aloft, Wales shirt gleaming brightly under the night sky. The whole ground was going bananas and the Germans couldn't take it. Their easy type of "beach soccer" became an irrelevance as Andy thumped the ball clear, Mark Hughes charged and challenged and Neville, well, Neville... He was a giant.

The intensity of the crowd was becoming alarming. He of the Wrexham shirt was "blue" in the face. My leg sported a three-inch gash from God knows where. At the final whistle I could have been amputated from the knee without so much as a downward glance. I was delirious.

I abandoned my seat in a race towards the pitch. I was only halted by the fact I was some twenty yards above it. Undeterred, I took to beating the boards in ecstasy as the Germans silently folded their flags. I hugged a total stranger. He hugged me back twice as hard. He could have been the leader of The Pencoed Jacks for all I cared. For once the whole of Wales was united. Awful night games with City were a distant memory. Anfield 77? Suddenly they all seemed worthwhile. Saturdays had at last justified themselves to me. I knew why I watched football. I was close to tears, I was close to ejaculation!

Get in there, a magic moment as Ian Rush fires Wales ahead. Final Score Wales 1 West Germany 0

I raced out of the ground to celebrate. I seized a discarded *South Wales Echo* cutting – "1-0 to Wales – Says Yorath" the headline. Oh, how true! I held it aloft like Moses with his tablet of stone. I danced and sang uncontrollably.

Back at The City club the air was heady. Nobody thought about whether or not Wales would qualify. We had beaten the best team in the world, that was all that mattered. We had all played our part. Next season I would be at Crewe and Barnet, but today we had beaten the world champions.

Oh, how we danced!

Down in a Tube Station at Midnight

It was 1977, London's punk-rock scene was setting the world alight as Wales ventured to the twin towers of Wembley to take on England. Five thousand Wales fans in a crowd of 48,000 boomed out the national anthem. Most of the 5,000, it seemed, were from Cardiff. That's not exactly true, but the memory was not absolutely reliable after this away day with the Barry Boys, monsters, it seemed, to a man.

England 0 Wales 1! "DISGRACE TO WALES Fans left behind" screamed the headlines from the *South Wales Echo* on Thursday, June 2nd 1977. Fear, bloodshed, violence, the whole sorry tale set out in full in the local papers. Angry coach drivers swearing, "Never again." Stranded sons far from home. It was a long, long time ago and far away. Ah yes, I remember it well.

The decision to embark on this fateful venture was taken whilst passing from The Horse and Groom public house to The Cottage sometime around Christmas in 1976. The air was festive, the world was gay (yes, you could say that word then). What could possibly go wrong? The answer, excluding the game, was simply everything.

The three revellers who left the Horse and Groom that beer-frenzied Christmas were two by the time we arrived at The Albert at noon on Tuesday, May 31st 1977. We ate a hearty breakfast of pasties and brown sauce complemented by Brains Dark before setting off to the dark streets of London Town. We decided to travel with the supporters' club on the "proper job" coaches that promised a quiet drive to London. On this mild spring afternoon, whilst walking to the pick-up point, I made the worst decision of my life. A charabanc pulled up and we received a warm invitation to board and travel to the game at a very reasonable and "knock-down" price. So, should we trundle on down Tudor Road as planned, full of Dark, or should we accept the offer to join this friendly looking outing from Barry? You guessed it. Of course we climbed aboard. Oh dear!

It soon became apparent that the entire coach was pissed. The first official toilet stop was at Howells Garage in Newport Road, some eight minutes after setting off. Every hooligan in Barry was standing outside the coach watering the wheels. In those far-off primitive days, in-coach loos were unheard of. As we set off again the driver, who was to play a major part in our day out, invited us to urinate out of the coach's open door as we sped along the M4. The contents of many bladders were emptied along the motorway to the accompaniment of "Scarlet Ribbons" from the back seats. I was in the presence of Cardiff City's Barry Boys. Oh dear!

Our next stop was Chievely Services on the M4, and as soon as we alighted from the coach the Barry Boys introduced themselves to their English cousins. In a few seconds one was naked and others staggered around the service area. A frail old lady picked her way through the madness and debris, the shop was empty and not a penny changed hands. Oh dear!

Now amidst all this chaos it must not be forgotten that this was to be one of Wales's greatest footballing days, a trip to the twin towers no less. We made it to the ground and those towers loomed in the distance, my first memory of the place. They stood majestically in the distance as we neared the fabled ground to park up for the evening. We made our way to a conveniently situated pub. An ashtray was soon collected as a souvenir, though I swear I never went inside. A coachload of Englishmen turned up, complete with the usual gestures and insults, very tiresome indeed. One of the Barry Boys was on the coach in a flash. Veggie, he was called. He removed his front teeth and entered the coach, grabbing the first person he could at the front. This chap also had his false teeth removed. Veggie emerged with his trophy, still toothless but unscathed. We left for the ground and I was terrified.

We soon spotted familiar faces from the Grange End, yes, 1977 was a long time ago. One in particular was swathed in a collection of scarves, including England ones. He was a stealer of Welsh flags. On seeing this, some Welsh supporters set upon him. However, on finding out he was Welsh they duly apologised for the blows already delivered. He replied, "Things aren't that simple boys." Then battered a few of them for even believing he was English.

I was being enlightened by the minute. We paid our £1.50 entry, made our way to the Welsh end and looked out on to the hallowed turf. A glorious sight! Three days earlier Manchester United had beaten Liverpool in the FA Cup final and now Don Revie's men were about to entertain us. They had a load of household names; we had Joey Jones and Dai Davies. Another five had turned out for Cardiff

City at some time or another: Leighton Phillips, Rod Thomas, Dave Roberts, Bryan Flynn, and Peter Sayer. Not forgetting Gabalfa bred, Terry Yorath, the midfield captain who held us together. Nick Deacy was up front, remember him? Wales battled and battled, cheered on by a large contingent of Welsh fans. The majority of the fans had an allegiance to one particular Welsh club, of course. Traditions die hard in south-east Wales.

In the 42nd minute Shilton fouled Leighton James in the box and the penalty was given. James himself stepped up and fired the penalty home. Wales were winning 1-0. To date this was the greatest moment of my life. All the pretend matches against the English played in the back gardens of Wales were coming true. I had scored hat-tricks in all these matches, let me tell you that, but on this occasion I was more than willing to accept the solitary goal as victory tonight. For the rest of the game I chewed my fingers and watched three efforts on the Welsh goal kicked off the line. Dai Davies took years off my life saving certain equalisers, and the captain Yorath was everywhere. After a lifetime of whistling I recall Sayer throwing his arms in the air and Welsh players jumping for joy. Wales had beaten England at Wembley. The last time had to be 1927. I missed that game, this was an historical first for Wales.

If the Barry Boys were lively before the game they were madness itself afterwards. Imagine their glee as the scent of victory filtered through their nostrils. They ran out of the stadium to spread the word to all and sundry. My own personal fortunes took a backward step at this point as two disgruntled home supporters set

Remember this strip? Modelled by Toshack.
England 0 Wales 1 1977

upon me while I was searching for our coach. They whipped off my scarf and boxed my ears good and proper, and I made the decision to quit the ring there and then. My record, fought one, lost one, a sound testament.

Finding our coach was becoming a full-time job. Numerous other coaches left the ground, leaving some equally foxed familiar faces in the rapidly emptying car park. The warm spring afternoon was now a cold, dark night. The unbelievable had happened; the driver had left without us. He had had enough and gone back to Barry. The trip to the game had been enough for any coach driver to put up with so he had left for an early tea, taking mine with him. He had left us stranded in London and my cherry cake was still on the coach! Oh dear.

Not to worry, there's the Barry Boys over there (oh dear!). They had got their second wind and were busy diverting traffic with temporary road signs. A nearby exclusive hotel was visited and the majority of the residents informed of the result by the Barry Boys. The Met Police were now present so, as we had managed to keep a low profile, I suggested to my fellow traveller, the luckless Gary, that we take God's speed to the train station. He agreed. We hitched to Paddington down the Harrow Road but there was not a lift in sight. We caught a taxi to the train station, and were left virtually penniless.

Paddington at midnight, tube and mainline, is short on entertainment. It's cold and lonely and there's no talent. But fear not, for the night was far from over. Through the mist came the Barry Boys complete with police escort, like a recurring nightmare. They too had come in search of the "milk train".

Did this mythical vehicle actually exist though? Was there really a train offering free lifts, warm milk and a warm bed to travellers in the middle of the night? In a word, no. The next train was at 7am. It was 1am, it was cold and I was on a station platform with 40 hooligans. Think about this when you're tucked up in bed tonight.

As Ali Baba and his forty thieves roamed the platforms of Paddington we stood near to a warm draught emitting from the tube station's entrance. There was nothing open except a Wimpy at the station. Gary informed me I would laugh about this in time to come. As I slept and shivered on BR's finest benches I doubted it. I still doubt it today.

Eventually, at 6am I think, the ticket office opened and we inched a step nearer to home. Our finances stretched to two half fares to Cardiff. We would worry about the ticket inspector later. At seven we were, indeed, in heaven. We were on the train back home, and despite the accompaniment of 40 oversized fourteen-year-olds we were in heaven. I had never been happier.

My scars were showing and my scarf had gone. I had been to hell and back and seen a 1-0 victory, let's not forget that. I was at the next three England v Wales games and we lost only once. There were 70,000 at Wembley in 1979 when Dwyer played, and in 1983 I met Ian Rush. Somehow it was not the same. We got home safely from each game after this and never again made the headlines – carefully planned mini buses from The Albert after 1977 saw to this. Wales never won again. I never got lost or beaten up, and I never had the company of Veggie and the Barry Boys again. I wonder where they are now. Do they remember that game, the night we spent together, the victory?

I do, I remember it well. Oh dear!

An Obsession... but I can explain

I was taken to my first football match long ago by my father. At the tender age of nine, having reached an appropriate level of maturity, my initiation was set for an evening at the second leg of the 1968 Welsh Cup final, as Cardiff City took on the might of non-league Hereford United. Nothing like starting at the bottom, eh?

John Charles appeared for Hereford, leaving my father in awe. Being little more than a tot, I could barely see this gentle giant of the game, but my father was over the moon. It was 30 years ago and he's dead now, but my father's pride in sharing the same stadium as his hero remains my overriding memory of the evening.

City won the match 4-1 to take the trophy 6-1 on aggregate. John Charles scored. I know all this, because I've looked it up. But I know that my father was in awe because I was there. Sometimes you just have to be there.

And so over the years our regular spot became the floodlight between the Bob Bank and the dark and cavernous Grange End. I was oblivious then to how my life would be changed, indeed, almost taken over by the events to unfold around these enormous structures. If I'd known, I'd have probably left at half-time against Hereford.

Actual games have faded from the mind now (though for some reason I always remember Ian McKechnie in goal for Hull City) but simply being at Ninian Park as the seventies opened is a memory which lingers to this day. The malady lingers on, you might say. Well, you might.

The giant fences which criss-cross the modern Ninian Park were nowhere to be seen back then, and shaven-headed masses of the infamous Cardiff City Skinheads would roam menacingly across from their natural habitat on the huge Grange End in search of, well, who knows what on the Bob Bank. (Why does the club's official literature always refer to it as the "Popular Bank"? I know of no one who calls it the Popular Bank. I digress.)

I was terrified to even look at these monsters, yet at the same time found them fascinating. "Watch the game!" barked my father as I gazed not at Ronnie Bird but at Big Frankie from Canton, while the endless army snaked its way past us in single file. It was to prove a defining moment. For the next 30 years the fortunes of the players would occasionally be rendered incidental as my obsession with what I wore to the game, where I stood, how I got there – with simply being a City fan – become just as important as the performances of Albert Larmour, Billy Ronson or a thousand others.

Before I continue the tale, a little clarification is required for the uninitiated. You see, the events that followed that first Welsh Cup final could probably only have gone the way they did at that precise period in the history of Cardiff City. I didn't plan to build my life around this team, I guess I was just in the right place – at the wrong time. My mate Gary is just a few years older than me and, without pausing for breath, he can still recite the names of the victorious City side which beat Real Madrid in 1969. Others haven't been back to Ninian Park since the sale of John Toshack. Whereas unfortunately – or fortunately depending on your enjoyment of this chapter – these great events somewhat passed me by. I remember Tosh, of course, but I doubt if I'd been to a dozen games before he set off for Anfield. Since that time I've seen him score a hat-trick for Wales against Scotland,

and score the winner for Swansea against City in 1980. I still can't decide if I love him or hate him.

My all time City XI would probably have Jimmy Gilligan and Carl Dale up front. I love 'em both. Two of us went to Oxford to see Gilligan's debut for Pompey after being sold by City in 1989/90, and I've got Cad Dale's autograph three times. Such things shape your views, you know?

Anyway, City's promotion failure of 1971 turned into relegation battles that would never end. My shiny schoolboy rosette became a Wrangler jacket and feather cut. I worshipped Willie Anderson coz he looked like George Best. John Buchanan passed me in St Mary Street once and I nearly fell over. I was hooked.

Not surprisingly, my father had long since lost interest in all this. Relegation battles against Crystal Palace (it always seemed to be Palace) surrounded by half the hooligans in South Wales held limited appeal I suppose. For me, it became life itself. One of my mates lived in Hengoed. He assured me, when I turned up in crombie with matching accessories of a hand-knitted City scarf with sewn on Wales badge, that all the skins in the valleys dressed like that. I felt socially accepted for the first time in my life.

Now this image of a switched-on, well trendy, Splott Boy has only one minor flaw. A technicality. Hardly worth a mention really. Well, you see, I simply wasn't hard. Skinny and small with an Adam Faith "Budgie" haircut, I'd have run a mile from any real aggro. All my mates had hard-sounding nicknames like Uggie, Smiffy or Gus. I was Weedy. No one's gonna spray "Weedy Rules OK" on the back of the Grange End are they. The macho culture has a lot to answer for I can tell you.

Boxing Day 1975 saw my first away match – Swindon Town. In those days Swindon and Bristol were the big local rivals and it seemed every teenager in Cardiff was running from the coaches to the ground in a longhaired mass of denim and tank tops. Why were we running? Well, who knows. No one was chasing us and, as far as I could tell, we weren't chasing anybody. But I ran with the crowd, intoxicated.

Despite my white, yellow and blue Leeds scarf with a Cardiff City Superfan sticker sewn onto it, City lost 4-0. Bonehead (no one went by their real name in my school) had promised me that everyone sang at away matches. He was right. I think our entire class went to Crystal Palace in 1976, where an Adrian Alston goal gave City victory in front of 25,604. I recall little of the game now, over twenty years later, but clearly remember singing the National Anthem and Joe's home-made "Mal eats Footballs" banner (Malcolm Allison – mouthy former manager). That season I went to 31 first team matches – including a specially arranged "friendly" against Bristol City to celebrate promotion for both sides. Both teams entered the pitch kicking free footballs to the crowd. Look out for a similar venture if Cardiff and Swansea go up together, eh?

Away games have always held a curious fascination. The more bizarre outings have included Bristol Rovers in the Anglo Scottish Cup, Cwmbran Town for a pre-season friendly and Halifax Town in midweek. Recently I boarded the supporters' club official minibus to Hartlepool on a Tuesday night in November, only for the game to be called off 40 minutes before kick-off while we drove through Darlington. Cardiff City paid for a free trip to the rearranged fixture, this time on a Tuesday night in February. We won 3-2 and I danced with Gareth Stoker's mum after he had scored the winning goal at our end. Two midweek trips to Hartlepool in the same season. Is this getting out of hand do you think?

By the eighties the adolescent Gang of 30 had become the Gang of Two. But between leaving school in 1975 and getting married in 1985, I doubt if I missed more than ten home games, and the giant "Sprukey" was at my side for each one. If either of us wasn't stood directly beneath the cameras on the Bob Bank every other Saturday, then something was up. You name 'em ... we've seen 'em.

I have seen City play every team in the league at home except Liverpool and West Brom. We watched gleefully as Peter Kitchen scored five against Cardiff Corries in the Welsh Cup, rejoiced as Billy Woof swept home a late winner in his only appearance against Middlesborough and grimaced as City lost at home to Weymouth while going for promotion in 1982. Why, we even took the afternoon off work to catch Peter Osgood's appearance for Southampton reserves against City's combination side circa 1979 – had to go in the Grandstand for that though, as the club didn't open the Bob Bank. Where's their sense of tradition?

After a while, things just became ridiculous. We'd meet in the Moorlands pub in Splott after "Football Focus" (neither of us still lived in Splott but there you go), catch a City Circle bus which took us halfway around Cardiff, to end up on exactly the same square yard of concrete as last time. A pasty was, of course, compulsory.

City contributed to this treadmill by staging an annual dogfight against relegation, only to escape in the last home game every year. Most people remember the long hot summers of their childhood in scenes reminiscent of an Enid Blyton novel. My early adulthood was one long winter where the Famous Five were City's Back Four, with Ron Healey in goal. If we lost at home the entire plot was ruined until the City Circle began the cycle again two weeks later.

Away games were even more extreme, the selection of each trip being based on formulae which would have taxed Einstein, or even John Motson. Had we been there before? How far was it? Would we get a beer and be back in time for a swift one in Cardiff afterwards? Was it an important game? Would City win?

In order to be assured of a decent seat on the coach from Ninian Park, Sprukey and I would (listen to this palaver!) each catch the Number 30 Newport to Cardiff bus (from different locations naturally), travel right the way across Cardiff to the station – including a walk down Tudour Road – turn up at Ninian Park at around 8.30am, only to head back across Cardiff via .. the road to Newport. Some weeks we'd go right past Sprukey's house!

But this itinerary took us to all manner of exciting outposts – Oldham (lost 2-1, Phil Dwyer scored); Orient (lost 4-1 with a Kevin Bartlett goal); Southampton (lost 3-2, I think Robin Friday scored 'em both). We also visited Bristol, Swindon (again) and Brentford. However, the only time our detailed criteria were fully met was at Exeter in January 1983 – beer beforehand, two-nil win for City courtesy of Bob Hatton and Jeff Hemmerman then back in the Ninian Park pub by 8 o'clock. And Andrew Dibble signed my programme! The worst trip was easily that to Wolves in the dying days of the 1985/86 season – we were attacked entering and leaving the ground, City lost 3-1 and both teams were relegated to the Fourth Division. It was bloody hard work I can tell you.

Sprukey – whose real name is Richard, by the way – abandoned

Cardiff City when they sold Kevin Bartlett. "There's no ambition there," he moaned. Perceptive fellow, eh? For the next few years I roamed the enormous Bob Bank like a nomad in search of a home. Oh, of course there'd be the occasional mate from work or reluctant girlfriend (my wife was treated to City v Swansea on Boxing Day morning once!) but it wasn't until the fanzine movement took root in the early nineties that I felt settled again.

Ah, now. This was the life. "O Bluebird of Happiness" – written by sad City fans for sad City fans. Had I died and gone to Heaven? No. But I went to Crewe, Walsall and Aldershot and wrote the adventures up for my public. I had reached my destiny. Torquay in midweek, Gillingham, Fulham, ah wot larks, eh Pip, wot larks.

Though I say so myself, our fanzine was extremely well written and not short of the odd classic at times. Ian the Fish's account of the 1991 trip to Germany versus Wales ("Diary of an Ayatollah Follower") is a true collector's item. Dylan Thomas wouldn't have had a look in I can tell you. I was "nostalgia man" and waxed lyrical about City's worst ever Haircuts XV (Steve Tupling, Andy Polycarpou, Mark Grew – you get the idea); a history of Wales's football kits from 1975 and a marathon chronology of the club's turbulent fortunes as reflected in the match programmes 1956 – 1992!

I still go down the City regularly, though not like in the glory, glory days when Weedy and Sprukey "shagged your women and drank your beer". But the obsession remains as bad. Four of us went to a night game in Brighton around five years ago – and were in a pub in Hove by 5 o'clock. England v West Indies was live on SKY and we all grew far too drunk far too quickly. At the game itself I danced gleefully in the rain on the open away terrace as 10-man City held on for a 5-3 away win. I was 35 years old!

As I say, all these stories and many more (I was hit in a graveyard at Southend, got hit by a brick against Spurs and once sprayed "Adar Glas" on the back of my Wrangler Jacket) could only have happened at this precise time in history. From around 1971 to ... well, now really, City have either been fighting desperate relegation battles led by Phil Dwyer, Jason Perry and Linden Jones, or mounting a stirring promotion challenge roared on by an army of loonies. The number of times City have finished comfortably in mid-table with nothing to play for can be counted on the fingers of one thumb. So every game has always mattered intensely. When Dave Bennett was sent off for fighting at Lincoln in 1983, it was first versus second. A City fan broke the clock at Pompey in the same season – both teams ended up being promoted and 20,000 fans crammed into Fratton Park. I doubt if any other team in the league has endured such a roller coaster of emotion, heartache, ecstasy and bedlam in their entire history. Nathan Blake could only have played for Cardiff City – a frustrating head-banger one minute, the greatest living Welshman the next. He is, for me, all the players we've ever had rolled into one. I love him.

I'm in my forties now, but signs of normal mature behaviour seem as far away as when I agreed with my father that we could be seen to favour the opposition in a long-forgotten match against Newport County because we were eating barley sugar! (Amber shirts, see.)

The way we were: the Cardiff City v Arsenal programme of 1927.

I have sons of my own to-day – and keep a scrapbook of all the games they go to. I've a photo of one doing the Ayatollah, aged four. The other one once made me pin up our Welsh flag at a pre-season friendly away at Inter CableTel! I don't know where he gets it from I'm sure. For my nephew's fifteenth birthday I made a huge banner saying "Llanedeyrn Bluebirds". Although we took it to a home game against Northampton (lost 2-1 if memory serves), it was simply too big for the Family Enclosure to accommodate.

And so it goes on. In March 1999 I spotted an enormous St David's cross flag strung up on the Grange

The way we looked: Cardiff City with the FA Cup after defeating Arsenal at Wembley in 1927

End at a 0-0 draw with Chester City. I simply have to have one to go with the Welsh flag on which I've now written "Caerdydd" in white letters. See if you can spot it next time that the game is not as riveting as you might hope. We cut the letters from self-adhesive paper that we then stuck on by hand. Me and the nephew took it to Peterborough on a cold day in January this year – lost 2-1 – and took turns running over to the fence to replace missing letters as they blew off across the terraces.

Thirty years from now you'll have forgotten all about the result at that Peterborough game, but, if you were there, you'll still recall the flag which said CA RDY D and the two nutters who scrambled around the steps chasing bits of paper. Like I say, sometimes you just have to be there.

Chapter 9

Clouds of Darkness, Clouds of Despair – Keeping a Weather Eye on Swansea City

Huw Bowen

Now and again you read a piece of football writing and have to take some time out to think about just how this individual has managed to tweak a few strings and make you draw breath. Huw Bowen, a Swansea City fan, is a professor at Leicester University and studies football amongst many other things. He writes about the weather in this piece, but does so eloquently and may just raise a smile or two as you read it. Enjoy Huw's view. I did.

Perhaps it is because the Swan, by nature, lives in a watery home; perhaps it is because Alan Curtis once walked on the stuff; or perhaps it is because Harry Griffiths and John Toshack performed the most unlikely miracle and turned the murkiest of waters into the sweetest tasting wine. Whatever the reason, Swansea City is, in my mind, always to be associated with close encounters of the very wettest kind. To put it at its most simple: think Swans, think rain; think Vetch, think clouds of darkness and despair.

I am sure that I am not alone in taking a view of the Swans which charts the club's fortunes over the last thirty years or so within terms of reference marked out by weather patterns and atmospheric conditions in south-west Wales, the rain capital of Britain. Others, of course, have sought their explanations and patterns elsewhere. I remember one fanzine article which argued with great conviction that the team's league position always bore an exact correlation to the meat content of the pasties on sale at the Vetch (bring back the bakers Davies' of Mumbles, all is forgiven). There are also those who suggest that the lamentable performance of successive generations of PA announcers lies at the very heart of all the club's problems over the years. But I have long taken the view that any follower of Swansea Town or City is quite capable, like me, of having water on the brain.

This is because our snapshot images and memories of the Vetch Field are more often than not shaped by recollections of long-forgotten games played out against a background provided by damp, dismal, windswept days and nights. Drizzle drifts past floodlight pylons across a quagmire pitch and into the faces of the poor deluded fools who sit in the East stand in the mistaken belief that they are somehow going to find shelter from the elements. Water cascades down the dolls' house roof of the Centre Stand, falling past broken guttering and eventually forming glistening pools on the red shale running track. On the pitch, white shirts turn brown, and would-be tacklers slither from the turf and into advertising hoardings. The Vetch, living up to its name, slowly becomes a muddy, churned-up vegetable patch. And all the time, silently and out of sight, the puddle that always forms between the gateposts at the exit from the North Bank grows into an enormous lake. It lies ready to claim hundreds more shuffling, grumbling victims who have not yet mastered the art of the thirty-foot leap from a standing start.

No doubt I look back through mist-tinted glasses, but the only break in this thirty-year rainy season came when the Swans were taking flight in Division One and game after game seemed to be played out before shirt-sleeved crowds in warm conditions and glorious sunshine. Alan Curtis destroyed Leeds in cricketing weather; Robbie James advanced on a retreating Spurs defence on a balmy late-Summer evening; and Gary Stanley launched a thirty-yard missile of a shot into the Manchester City net in the bright spring sun. Maybe I have now wallowed in the nostalgia brought about by too many video re-runs of 'Swansea City: The Golden Years', but I am convinced that not a drop of rain fell on south-west Wales between August 1981 and May 1982. Tosh even fixed the weather. Golden Years and golden days, but then someone switched the lights off again.

Contrast all this with times before and since, and think of Hull City, Rotherham United, Workington Town, and Doncaster Rovers. The storm clouds gather in the mind, the outlook darkens, and it begins to rain. To the surface rise mildewed memories of bleak days, with little entertainment, false dawns and no hope. For me the Vetch

Field has become a theatre of wet dreams (no crude pun intended), and an even wetter reality. The games that stick in the memory are those which have been played out against a dark background of hail, snow, and torrential rain, and at times the only missing climatic ingredients are Wagnerian thunder and lightning above Townhill. Such fixtures that are perhaps easiest to recall are some of the biggest post-Toshack occasions: the Bournemouth 're-birth' game of 1986; the West Brom play-off match; and most recently, of course, the West Ham Cup replay. All were viewed through a watery curtain. But there are hundreds of others – routine league fixtures – lurking in the recesses of all of our minds. Conjure them up for yourself and see!

The away day, too, is now routinely an open-terraced, feet-numbing, rain-sodden, point-less experience that defies rational explanation to family, friends, and colleagues. Deeply etched on my soul is a 6-0 hammering on a glistening, sodden pitch on a dismal Darlington day. We were 4 or 5-0 down at half-time, when we were awarded a penalty – only for Colin Pascoe to put the ball not only over the bar but out of the ground as well. Only last season a 4-1 reverse in driving rain at Cambridge was partially enlivened by the fact that there was so much mud on offer for players and spectators alike that Tony Bird felt obliged to present some of it to a linesman from a range of ten yards or more. And Hartlepool, Hartlepool, Hartlepool. If only I could sing, with some conviction, of the Swans, 'You are my sunshine, my only sunshine, you make me happy when skies are grey'. Unfortunately, I can't ever quite bring myself to do it.

It was not always like this. Earliest memories of Swansea Town and the Vetch Field conjure up images of vivid colours, brightness, action, speed and, above all, a rich green pitch. Catching a first glimpse of the seemingly expansive playing surface, with the tinny strains of 'The Woody Woodpecker Song' playing in the background, was a defining, almost breathtaking moment. Even now the sight of the pitch still has the capacity to quicken the pulse and raise expectations at ten to three on a Saturday afternoon. Unfortunately, however, the colour and brightness did not last. They first disappeared, temporarily, during the late sixties when the straw bales stored, quite bizarrely and recklessly, underneath the North Bank caught fire and smoke billowed across the ground, obscuring pitch and stands alike. The crowd, cheerfully unaware that they were now standing on top of a potential towering inferno, provided an appropriate accompanying chorus of 'Swansea Town is burning down'. But the clouds closed in permanently a short time later when I seemed to enter a completely unfamiliar bleak world. This was not yet the long dark tunnel of adolescence in which inexplicable things happened such as the exchange of two hundred Swans programmes for a couple of Barclay James Harvest albums (no excuses, but this was the early 70s when strange things happened to all of us). Rather this was a glamour-free world of lower division soccer entirely devoid of any colour and light.

The entry into this black hole occurred in March 1970 when, touched by promotion fever, I attended a midweek fixture against the late, lamented Bradford Park Avenue. What was unusual about this occasion (a 5-0 victory with Herbie Williams scoring a hat-trick) was that I did not sit in my usual spot on the low wall that runs in front of the North Bank. Instead, an accompanying uncle took me for the first time into the upper tier of the Double Decker stand, where spectators sat on bench seats and stamped their feet on a worryingly shaky wooden floor. This produced the disorientation that always accompanies such a move away from familiar spectating territory, but it also gave me my first 'aerial' view of a pitch which had been saturated by the constant heavy rain which continued to sweep in from the sea during the game. Having been used to watching proceedings from a position level with or even below the playing surface, and always finding myself looking up into the bright floodlights, it came as something of a shock to realise that things were not as they had always seemed. The centre of the pitch itself resembled a swamp, with patches of mud joining together large pools of standing water. In fact, the only evidence of any grass at all was to be found on the flanks patrolled by Carl Slee and Vic Gomersall (who surely must have possessed the deepest chest and thickest thighs of any of the players who have ever turned out at the Vetch). The proceedings were played out in a murky semi-darkness that was so gloomy that it was easy, indeed fascinating, to watch the near-constant lighting and re-lighting of matches and cigarettes by fans standing on the North Bank.

Although I was to return to my position on the North Bank for the next match, the effect of that visit to the Double Decker was to remain with me long after details of the game itself disappeared from view. Against the prevailing seventies trend, the Vetch was transformed from a colour set into black and white, and it is the watery, mono-chrome images that are now fixed in my mind. A few shafts of bright-ness are to be found, such as the pre-season friendly against Accra Hearts of Oak or some of the grotesque and garish programme cover designs and team strips that have been put before us over the years. But, 1981-2 apart, these are insignificant exceptions to the general rule which suggests that if you adopt the Swans as your team you must also be prepared to take on the weather and the forces of dark-ness which can combine to do some very funny things to your mind.

It would be reassuring to believe that these dark Swansea clouds at least had some sort of silver lining with them. But they appear to have a Silver Shield instead and, as close observers of the Vetch Field ba-rometer will tell you, this is not quite the same thing. Oh well, it seems like rain again.

Chapter 10

Kick it out!

Anonymous contributors

There comes a time when the moaning and, indeed, the laughter have to take a step backwards. I hesitated over including these pieces, but after a lot of thought felt that they had their place. The writers of these contributions took the time to put their views across and I felt this was the right forum. The subject is emotive – racism in the game. And not only in Wales.

Maybe after reading these contributions you should pull a cold one from the fridge and think about your own experiences at football matches, and ask yourself the question, "What did I do about it?" Thought-provoking or just provoking?

There has been a definite increase in the number of racial taunts at grounds throughout the country in recent years, even though the majority of football fans are now in no position to argue that they have not been educated enough. This startling report on the state of the game in Wales followed visits to various grounds, ignore it at your peril. The message here is still, "Kick it out."

Introduction

Keith Haynes

When you're sixteen and stupid it's easy to be brainwashed into thinking that certain things are acceptable. Politics are often extreme and any form of group involvement presents the authorities with a youthful exuberance that is very hard to control. In the seventies right-wing literature was freely available outside many football grounds. Leaflets claiming all manner of birthrights were handed out to the vociferous teens on the terraces, and a generation of football fans found themselves screaming at black players just because of their colour. Were you one of those people? And more importantly how did those unchecked days of patriotism affect you and your prejudices later, when you took your place at your favourite football ground?

When that generation of teenagers became parents taking their children to football there was much work to do. A parent's opinion about someone's colour or origin will obviously influence a child, until he or she is educated in some way or another to reject this view. Football is doing its bit, but many believe it's a token effort because not enough is seen to be done. After all, the owners of these clubs needed educating too, and many turn a blind eye to the monkey noises and taunts that come from the terraces every Saturday. Take a look at some of the opinions here and make your own mind up. Have we really come so far or underneath the facade is there a bigger evil lurking? Football is, after all, a major influence on many of tomorrow's police officers, social workers, solicitors and politicians. Here are the facts from some spectators, and they don't make pleasant reading.

TW writes about her view of the game from the away end at Ninian. An end that held 2,000-plus Swansea fans for a midday kick-off. She felt that there was more to this game than just a Welsh Derby for the SKY TV cameras.

Cardiff City v Swansea, April 1999

I've followed Swansea now for three years, since Jan Molby first came to the club. With two of my friends I have travelled to a lot of grounds with other Swans fans. What I have found hard to accept this season is the taunting from fellow supporters that I have witnessed at games, at Southend and Cardiff especially. I witnessed the Southend goalie being racially abused because of his colour and at Ninian in April I saw real racism and the kind it breeds for the first time.

We had to travel on coaches from Swansea to this game and it was a lottery regards who you travelled with. My friend and I were not in the normal company so we were a little concerned about who would be on our coach. As we left Swansea a group of supporters who clearly all knew each other were bragging about their exploits when up against Cardiff supporters. They were revelling in battles won and victories gained. I was not surprised to hear this at all; there is a real hatred for Cardiff from the people of Swansea, it has always been the same. But their conversation soon turned to John Williams, an ex-Swansea player now at Cardiff. These guys were very abusive about his colour, and I really can't write the things they said about him. Suffice to say they were all old enough to know better, some of them were well over thirty years of age. I saw them later in the ground. They were with some supporters from Leeds United and I really don't think any of them watched the game at all. They just talked in a small group and seemed really unhappy about the fact they couldn't get to the Cardiff City supporters. They seemingly lost their interest in the game. I know a lot of people take in a lot of things at football, some of it is nasty. I just had this overriding sense of fear when I was near to this group of people, they oozed hatred and violence. I haven't seen any of them since and really hope I don't have to again. If this had been my first game I wouldn't have gone again.

BT was at the same game and writes of his view of racism from the Bob Bank at Ninian Park.

I've been a City fan for thirty-two years and I have seen the racist violence of earlier years many times before. We all know it's unacceptable to many football supporters but it's very evident today. I travelled to see City play a London side a few months back and their black winger had a tremendous amount of abuse from many City fans in the crowd. So much abuse that I had a word with a young lad who was dishing out monkey chants to this player. He laughed at me and said, "It's nothing, we're just putting him off." Now I had never thought about it like this, but this kid knew what he was doing was wrong but he still persisted in the chanting in the hope that the player would be put off his game. I couldn't accept that to give him so much abuse would put him off his game, but there were clearly many there who thought it would. I would say that the majority giving him this abuse were not racists. Some were just joining in, some, as this kiddie said, putting him off, but there were some there who were intent on promoting racial hatred of all black and even English players. I could see them so why didn't the stewards? What powers do you actually need to rid us of these idiots?

At the Swansea game at Ninian we were presented with a vast number of Union Jacks from the Swansea end and I saw what I believed were Nazi salutes from some of the Swans support. I also saw the same from a small group on the Bob Bank. Now nobody actually did anything this time and it's hardly surprising. This group was very aggressive and anyone who confronted them, City or not, would have been set upon – that much I am sure of. I can't accept that nothing is being done about this behaviour, but why does it still exist? You don't see it when we play a game away when only a few hundred City turn out so why the hell should we put up with it for big games. The police and stewards should stamp on it so the majority of us can enjoy watching the games and the team we love. It's spoiling it for us.

DS follows a small Welsh League side and his story maybe takes a step closer to explaining why this behaviour continues, even at grounds where only 120 or so supporters attend.

I've followed my local town side for about twenty years. In this time we have flirted with success, but in the main we amble on and have even gone out of the Welsh League in recent times. We have a support at home of about 100 to 150, but we have been known to take 500 away from home, especially for a Welsh Cup tie a few years back. These matches are when we have most of our problems. Our location means that we get a lot of Cardiff and Swansea idiots turning up for big games, we are very much in the middle of these two cities.

The experience of racism I want to describe was at a game I went to at the beginning of the 1997/98 season. A visiting black player was having a very good game and, I have to say, I looked forward to seeing him receive the ball. He was quick and we don't see many players on form like this every week. During the first half a couple of local kids were taunting him and shouting at him. I knew their fathers and at this time they were not being over the top with their comments. Just booing him and shouting comments such as, "You're rubbish". Their fathers were standing behind them – the luxury at our ground is that you can buy a pint and watch the game whilst you have a drink, nobody says anything for normal games.

In the second half this player scored two goals in the space of a few minutes, I clapped them because both were very well taken from outside the area. After this the kids who were giving him stick changed their tune to chants of "black bastard". They were screaming at him and I was very embarrassed. I said to one of their fathers, whom I thought I knew quite well, that their taunts were not on. I couldn't believe it when he just laughed at me. "Leave it alone now," he said to me, "they are doing nothing wrong." But they were I explained to him, they were spoiling my enjoyment of the game and that of others too. He got very aggressive and shouted that the player was a nigger and deserved the abuse, and anyway they were used to it.

I couldn't accept this and informed the club of my experiences that afternoon. What did they do? Nothing at all. Should I be surprised by this? This man still attends games but refuses to stand by my wife and me. Every time a black player plays against us he smiles and looks at me, pointing him out and laughing. I haven't seen his kids since, but what can I say? If the parents can't educate these urchins then what bloody hope do we have? I don't think you will ever get rid of the animosity towards black players at games – that is, of course, unless he is playing for us! The odd thing here is that the black player that played so well against us before now plays for the club, that's why I won't say who he is or where I am from, though some of you will guess. And the only chink of light here is when he has scored for us. Then and only then do I catch the eye of the individual who points and laughs at him because of his colour, except this time it's my turn, and for the right reasons.

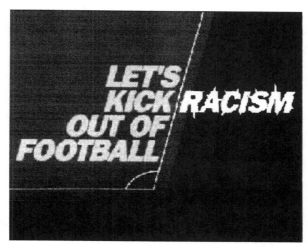

Comment

Keith Haynes

We have received other stories about racist abuse at games in Wales, but it's not something that you will encounter at every game. I have witnessed clear abuse of black players this season at Swansea, it's documented and the club is attempting to stamp it out. Maybe the first thing they should do is put the "Kick out Racism" signs facing those who involve themselves in this sort of pastime. A prosecution or two for racial chanting wouldn't go amiss here either.

It's a sad day when supporters are in fear of standing up for what they believe in, especially when we at Swansea have had our fair share of black players over the years. These players are often very good at their trade and receive no abuse at all when they play in Swansea's colours. But what do they think when they hear this sort of abuse? It must have an effect on them, and it can't be a good one.

The generation that accepted those leaflets in the seventies must now be persuaded to educate their children to see that this behaviour is not acceptable. Those reluctant to change require your very best attention if the game in Wales is to continue to flourish. The clubs, the fans, the part-timers – all have a part to play. Even those clubs that find it funny to have chants of "sheep-shaggers" go unchecked in their grounds when Welsh clubs visit them! It's a national problem and one that will not go away as long as it's tolerated and allowed to happen. Football by its own definition breeds rivalry: two sides, two teams, two sets of values and often from different sides of the country. But it doesn't need more division, it doesn't need more abuse. Supporters themselves must be prepared to do something about this. If they accept it, the teams concerned will never flourish and those that they want to sit or stand next to won't be there for the next game. Kick it out!

Postscript: Since I completed this piece a 30-year-old Swansea fan has been convicted of a racist offence at a football match. He is serving one year in prison and received a three-year ban from all football grounds in England and Wales.

Chapter 11

A Rant from West Wales

Paul Ashley-Jones

Paul Ashley-Jones wrote a splendid piece for the first book – "A Short Message from Carmarthen". His follow-up is, in his own words, a rant – pretty apt as he is a Swansea fan who also enjoys following the success of his local club side. So, a rant from West Wales to touch a few more nerves.

It's been one of those seasons for the Carmarthen-based football fan. A season of "what if?" "if only", and "Oh God, I need a drink", as both Swansea City and Carmarthen Town contrived to fall at the second-last and final hurdles respectively.

The majority of Swans fans will look back on a season where progress was made on the field. This was the year when watching the Swans actually became fun again as opposed to something simply to be endured. Our FA Cup run was a real crack as each match in turn – Millwall, Stoke, West Ham (away) and West Ham (home) – bettered the last. The atmosphere at Upton Park was as good as I've ever experienced in a football match. My enduring memory is of the sound of mobile phones after Jason Smith had scored, with people ringing their wives, mums and kids, desperate to share the news. The chap behind me rang his mate, a Cardiff fan watching their game at Ninian Park. All good things come to an end but we ran Derby close in the fourth round and deserved a replay at their place. The cup run gave all Swans fans a taste of the high life again and, with tickets for the West Ham and Derby games capable of being sold twice over, a glimpse of what the club could achieve given the opportunity.

Off the pitch the jury is still out on owners Silver Shield. Call us cynics, but their promised land of promotions and a new stadium still seems little more than a pipe dream. I'm sorry if I sound negative, but having Doug Sharpe as your owner, chairman, nemesis for most of your Swans supporting life does tend to colour your judgement. Their handling of the cup tickets didn't help either. Still, the commercial side of the club has improved no end and the investment in youth will pay dividends in the near future. And don't forget Cyril the Swan. What can I say about Cyril? Well nothing really, he's beginning to get on my nerves to be honest.

In the league, inconsistency ruled, with the club prone to throwing away two points, particularly at home. Only one club, those footballing giants Halifax, did the "double" over us but we could only manage the same against Barnet and Hull. In the end it was shock to lose to Scunthorpe in the play-offs. I think the manager, players and fans expected to get to Wembley and win. Truth is we'd have struggled badly in the Second Division without serious team strengthening and whoever does go up (Scunthorpe or Orient) will come straight back down. Next season will be the real test for Hollins. Nice bloke, good man manager, but can he pick a player? Molby couldn't. Hollins has yet to sign a player since becoming manager (no wonder our chairman loves him!), with the majority of this season's success stories (Bound, Smith, Cusack, Howard and Thomas) having been signed by Alan Cork. Mind you, he also gave us Newhouse and Hartfield and failed to sign Carmarthen's Delaney, so don't hold your breath Brighton.

So what of Carmarthen Town's season? People are quick to scorn the League of Wales, but if ever there was proof of the positive effect it has had on Welsh football then Carmarthen Town is it. Languishing in the lower regions of the Welsh leagues and virtually bankrupt, the creation of the League of Wales gave the town the spur to get behind its football club. Following a lot of hard work, the last few seasons have seen the club rise to enter and become one of the best supported teams in the League itself. Sights this year were very much on a place in the top seven and qualification for next season's FAW Premier Cup. However, the season started poorly under former Swan and Welsh international John Mahoney. A smashing man but not the driving force the club needed. He felt his weakness was indecisiveness, but he was never really sure. By the time Tomi Morgan was appointed manager his only remit was to ensure the club avoided relegation. But he did better than that. Much, much better.

From beating Barry in Morgan's first game in charge, Carmarthen never really looked back: climbing up the table while marching onto the Welsh Cup final. In the end the club finished one place short of qualification for next season's FAW Premier Cup. However, with fellow Welsh Cup finalists Inter CableTel already assured of qualifying for Europe via the League of Wales, by defeating Conwy at Newtown in the other semi, Town were assured of a place in Europe next season. Or so we thought. By the time of the final the goalposts (if you'll excuse the pun) had been moved. So had the ground for that matter. The final became an all or nothing game for Carmarthen. Win and it was a place in the UEFA Cup and in the FAW Premier Cup; lose and they got nothing. And I mean nothing. The Welsh Cup isn't sponsored, so neither the winners or the losers get a penny from the FAW.

Despite the match being played at Merthyr, the Carmarthen fans outnumbered the Inter supporters by at least ten to one. The game was poor but roared on by an extra time non-stop chant of "Tomi Morgan's Barmy Army". (Well, it wasn't exactly a roar. There were three of us singing, all a bit drunk and embarrassing to be honest. And if my father-in-law, Town's Secretary, ever finds out I was one of them he'll probably ban me for life.) Town scored with only a few minutes of extra time to go – and promptly conceded the equaliser. And lost on penalties after leading that as well. Bummer, eh!

The whole Welsh Cup final business brings me on to the rant referred to in the title of this chapter. The whole thing was a shambles from start to finish. Wales's historic cup competition, steeped in tradition. Can the FAW get a sponsor for it? What do you think? By preventing the league clubs and Merthyr, Newport and Colwyn Bay from entering they have seriously devalued the Cup's appeal (well okay, Colwyn Bay's exclusion probably hasn't had that much of an impact). Not our fault cry the FAW, it's UEFA's decision. Well, have they ever tried to fight that decision? And if these clubs are banned from the Welsh Senior Cup (to give it its full title) why are they allowed to enter the Welsh Youth Cup year after year? (Good win Swans, by the way.) Instead, the FAW seem happy to put their name to a pointless BBC-sponsored competition. If this money could be put into the Welsh Cup, and all Welsh clubs were allowed to enter, it could return to the prestigious competition it once was.

Okay, so the Cup isn't what it used to be and there's no sponsorship or prize money. At least Town qualified for Europe by getting to the final. Oops, no, remember the FAW got that wrong as well. Sorry

Who would have thought that a big bird by the name of Cyril would dominate Welsh football in 1999?

about that, chaps. Except they couldn't even say that, could they? Have you ever heard the FAW apologise for anything? The remaining consolation was that the players would play at Ninian Park, a Football League ground on which the Welsh international team played on numerous occasions. Well, no actually. Cardiff changed their minds, or the FAW forgot to book it. Whatever. After much panic and huffing and puffing the final was arranged for Merthyr a few days before it was due to be played. To their credit Carmarthen Town took each of these setbacks with good grace and went on determined to enjoy their day. If the FAW could act with half as much professionalism then Welsh football would be in a much healthier position than it is today.

Just how much longer do the supporters of football in Wales have to put up with these people clinging to power like some Eastern European dictatorship? Times have changed but not our beloved football association. No sponsorship gained for our national league and cup competition. Thousands lost on trying to force clubs like Merthyr and Newport into a league they didn't want to join. Arbitrary fines and censures for any club who dares to question or criticise their wisdom. What about the latest £19,000 fine for the Swans because a couple of idiots ran onto the pitch during the Brighton game? How is that supposed to help matters? How will that make it safer to attend football matches? It won't, of course, but it certainly will help towards the cost of sending FAW officials on nice trips abroad, subsidise a few lunches and pay their motor mileage allowance.

Am I being unfair? Possibly, but how do we know? Do we ever see job descriptions for these people, terms of reference for their bloody committees? Of course not, they wouldn't stoop to sharing such information with irrelevant people like us, even if it existed (which it probably doesn't). Is it any wonder then if we're cynical, particularly when they continually get everything wrong?

Okay, rant over. So that was the season that was in West Wales. Our friends from the east did rather better with both Cardiff City and Newport AFC getting promotion. We're not bitter though, and wish Newport all the best for next season. And what of next season? Promotion for the Swans, a finish in the top three and European qualification for Carmarthen, and mass resignations and restructuring in the FAW. Personally, I'd settle for two out of three.

Chapter 12

Updates from Come on Cymru!

Some of our original contributors were keen to share more of their passionate or quirky (or both) views on Welsh football, and reaction to their first accounts made me suspect that readers would welcome more recent news. So here goes.

Jonathon Taylor kicked off *Come on Cymru!* with his story of how he found himself supporting Swansea City over 27 years. Now, three years later, it's 30 years. You didn't expect him to change, did you? His first offering was inspiring; he briefly updates you as to the position now.

Twenty-Seven Years in a Black and White Scarf – The Sequel

"Anything is possible..." When I first wrote those words I had no idea how prophetic they would prove to be. Indeed, not even Mystic Meg could have foreseen the frequency with which the door of the Swans managerial office (known to some of us as the Kevin Cullis Memorial Portal) would open and close, with no less than three managers paying the price of failure, naiveté, or downright stupidity.

The current incumbent, however, has gone some small way towards restoring the positive element of possibility at the Vetch. Come the final reckoning of his time at Swansea (and come it will ... death, taxes, and the Swans manager's job), if for nothing else, John Hollins will be fondly remembered as the architect of the 1998-99 FA Cup run, specifically for the two epic contests with Premiership West Ham United. If you could bottle and sell the atmosphere at the Vetch after the final whistle of the 1-0 replay victory over the Hammers, you would be a very wealthy person ... I'd certainly buy a crate.

So, now at the milestone (millstone?!) of thirty years in a black and white scarf, and a few more "I was there" matches along the way, I have one last confession to make. If and when the Swans ever aban-

Super Stu' crosses and Jason Smith scores for Swansea City at Upton Park.
Memories like this are worth the thirty-year wait.

don the Vetch for pastures new (the much mooted but ever-distant Molfa stadium, mayhap?), I am going to 'acquire' a piece of the Vetch, come hell or high water. The place has, effectively, been my second home, and whenever I move home I take a memento with me. Mind you, whatever it is I'll have it exorcised, just in case the ghost of Tommy Smith comes with it...

Colin Mansley still furthers his Chester City point of view via the fanzine pages of "Hello Albert". He lives in Birmingham and has followed Chester City for many years. His first offering was an exact account of Chester City, a club that has a ground bisected by the English/Welsh divide. This update from Colin will be well received by the Chester City congregation, and they just had to be included. Wrexham fans would never have forgiven us if they were not.

Prodigal's Progress

Gary Bennett's return for his third spell with Chester began auspiciously as he bagged thirteen goals in the first sixteen matches of the season. Then his past seemed to catch up with him. Back in 1987, when Gary was in his first spell with us, he was involved in a tackle with a Sheffield Wednesday player, Ian Knight, which virtually ended the latter's career. It was a reckless tackle born, I feel sure, more out of zeal than intent to injure – but it was captured by the television cameras and ten years later was used in the lawsuit brought by Knight against Bennett and Chester City. An out-of-court settlement with which Knight was reportedly "delighted" was the final outcome. I dread to think what the club's insurance premium became as a result.

At about the same time as this City drew the old enemy (seven letters beginning with "W" – or eight letters if you use the Welsh spelling) in the fourth round of the FA Cup. Another horrendous moment involving Chester was captured on TV as City bowed out tamely in one of the most subdued derbies in living memory. With the scores at 0-0 Benno had a brilliant opportunity to score but fluffed it. While Bennett fraternised with his erstwhile colleagues from Wrexham after the match, City fans were livid at the lack of passion shown by their team. "What a disgrace! A local derby and not even one booking," was one typical, if cynical, comment.

Another Fine Mess

A couple of weeks previously, an ordinary looking League match with Swansea had become the prelude to eighteen months of further heartache and turmoil for the already long-suffering fans of Chester. I was in a hotel bedroom on a Friday night, at the opposite end of the country to Swansea – traumatic memories of a play-off defeat the previous May and the most intimidating atmosphere I have ever experienced at a football ground have made me take evasive action ever since. Was it coincidence or an unconscious association that the hotel I was visiting was named The Swan? I flicked on the teletext. There was a message saying that Chester's match at the Vetch Field looked likely to be postponed because part of the ground had been declared unsafe.

The match was indeed postponed but was then hastily rearranged for the following Wednesday at Chester instead of the Vetch. This seemed to make absolutely no sense at all – the short notice meant there would be a poor attendance. We were later told that Chester had been keen to host the game because of "severe cash flow problems". Sure enough a winding up order from the Inland Revenue was announced shortly afterwards. The rest of the season was spent staving off the taxman and other creditors until the sale of three players for a combined total of £500,000 seemed to save the day. Mark Guterman, the chairman, seemed to think so and made effusive noises in the press, thanked supporters, players and Kevin Ratcliffe for their patience and announced that he had put together a rescue package for the club.

It appeared, however, that such a rescue was to be effected without another penny of Mr Guterman's money. Still bills were not being paid, Ratcliffe famously had to pay the local water board £5,000 out of his own pocket before a pre-season friendly with Tranmere could go ahead. A players' strike was averted at the last minute when their long overdue wages were handed over at a motorway service station prior to a friendly with Everton. Another winding up order was posted, this time by the club's own firm of solicitors - for an unpaid bill relating to the last winding up order. The catalogue is almost comical if it were not that the club I love was being dragged towards bankruptcy.

The Greatest Match of All Time

So, almost a year on from that fatefully rearranged match with Swansea, we were due to play them again on 17th October 1998, not knowing whether the club would be wound up in the High Court the following Monday. It was billed as possibly Chester's last ever match and the newly formed Independent Supporters' Association (ISA) drummed up as much support as possible to swell the gate to twice its usual size. The well organised, if devious, City fans subsequently managed to sway a poll conducted by a national magazine to get what was, in the event, a rather dull 1-1 draw voted "The Greatest Match of All Time". An editorial meeting vetoed City v Swansea in favour of the equally emotionally charged England World Cup win of 1966. And City continued to exist – in administration.

The achievements of Chester's ISA during months of crisis have been nothing short of superb and have given all their fans good reason to be proud. They have petitioned the Football League headquarters, and lobbied Parliament. Tony Banks, Minister for Sport, came to meet them. Money raised by the supporters and players (former goalie Grenville Millington donated his old jersey for auction and it raised £430) has helped keep the club afloat. The ISA organised another "Fans United" event – supporters of clubs from all over the country flocked to the Deva for City's match with Brighton and Hove Albion (another club which has known financial crisis and exile). That Friday night in January 1999 was brilliant. There were supporters from Portsmouth, Sheffield United, Frankfurt and many other places – even Manchester United! All were there out of solidarity with Chester's plight and that of other clubs like them. Lincoln City fans came equipped with their World War Two air-raid siren and its surreal warning pervaded the air every time there was a corner. Oxford United fans brought their scarf made up of one from all ninety-two League clubs (Wrexham included) and this was paraded around the pitch at half-time. A town hall reception followed the match and impassioned speeches on behalf of Chester, Brighton, Oxford and others were made. It felt good to be a Cestrian and a football supporter that night.

At the time of writing the future of the Chester City FC is still unresolved. No sugar daddy has come along offering to bankroll the club.

So as you read this Chester might be playing in the North West Trains League Division Two (quaint but obscure), the League of Wales (doubtful), or the Football League (please). Whatever the case, because of the spirit of the fans, I'm certain that there will be a Chester City FC and I'll still be there – third crush barrier from the left.

Kevin Ratcliffe has since resigned from the managers post at Chester City.

David Naylor or Dave the Weatherman as he is affectionately called by his fellow Gloucester Jacks, is our final contributor to *Come on Cymru!* to be recalled to the squad. He can be easily identified on any terrace and his account here is as purposeful as his first.

From the Table Top Stadium to Wembley Stadium

The paradise was revisited three years later and was almost within grasp a further two years down the line, but until then the roller coaster ride of emotions that only Swansea City could provide had to be endured.

My mum is a very superstitious person. There are many things that she will and won't do in pursuit of good luck – my dad is completely the opposite. As for me, well in this aspect I'm a fence sitter but I wouldn't walk under a ladder unless I had to! Looking back on the last five seasons, however, I'm beginning to wonder if the 'black cat' and 'ladder' brigade know something I don't.

In my job I have to make predictions all the time, some for an hour ahead, others for a week ahead. When things go wrong, one can always point to a "turning point". This is exactly the case with the Swans in the past five years – the "turning point" has always been at the end of October, specifically around the 28th-31st.

With the Autoglass Trophy well and truly locked in the cabinet, we all looked forward to a great, eventful season in 1994/95. We weren't disappointed! After a rather shaky start, mostly draws and defeats, along came **October 29th** and a 2-0 defeat of Peterboro'. Thereafter we lost only three games in the next eighteen. These included the FA Cup run in which we dismissed the 'Hersham boys 2-0 in the fog of suburban London, brushed aside Bashley on a breezy, sunny Sunday afternoon in the New Forest 1-0, beat Middlesboro' away 2-1 after a replay and then went to St James's Park, Newcastle. What a day! The 4,000 of us there that day sang our hearts out, and after the final whistle a certain Mr Keegan was tipping us for promotion after a valiant battle in which we were sunk 3-0 by a Kitson hat-trick. My abiding memory of the day was after the game as both sets of fans sang each other's praises – football united.

Yet more excitement was to come that season as we reached seventh position on the 7th March – a night I'll never forget. This was not only because we thrashed the bluebirds 4-1 in the snow at the Vetch with an orange ball, but because I drew the short straw and drove our minibus back to Gloucester. The first time that I had ever driven a minibus! The snow-covered M4 didn't help, neither did the headlights on the bus which were like something out of _Saturday Night Fever_, producing a marvellous flashing light show on the snow-covered ground! The piss stop at Sarn services was just that – the place was closed down but with the security cameras still rolling. Seventeen people, allegedly (!), paraded the finer parts of their anatomy and proceeded to wash windows and melt the snow! Full Monty it wasn't but something interesting for the security manager to view the following morning, nevertheless. I didn't get in until 3am the following morning and was then up for work at 6am. My wife had even phoned the police, fearing something terrible had happened. If you're reading this, Darren, I hope Karen has forgiven you – silly bugger forgot his house keys!

The following Saturday we were on that minibus again – fortunately it was daytime and I wasn't driving. With 10 men for most of the game we beat the blues 1-0 at St Andrew's. The second half was like something out of the Alamo as we barely got out of our own half. I counted 22 corners for Brum but the look on Jasper Carrott's face at the end was something to behold! After this epic performance, normal business was resumed and we gently slipped downwards to finish in 10th place.

The season of 1995-96 was the nadir of recent times. We were second after the first three games and 22nd at the end. After October 28th, there was only one win until January 20th. We saw five managers at the Vetch, including the 7-day reign of one Kevin Cullis. During the home defeat by Swindon on February 10th, the now collectors'

item from the Swansea City songbook echoed round the North Bank –
'Kevin Cullis's Black and White Army'!

The masochistic tendency latent inside me showed its hand on
November 18th. The previous Saturday I stood on the terraces at Cra-
ven Cottage and watched us get trounced 7-0 by Fulham. Fortunately,
the Shrews put 10 or 12 past Marine in another FA Cup tie so we were
spared most of the humiliating headlines. On November 18th it was
Gresty Road, Crewe, where the 4-1 defeat was made a little more pal-
atable by a seat under cover and a toilet with a bar of soap and a hand
towel! Something, I suspect, that will never be seen at Swansea. Jan
Molby, a gentleman if ever there was one, arrived at the end of February and nearly saved us from the drop. At last we started playing with
some confidence, which augured well for the future.

The following season, 1996-97, was when paradise was revisited.
Being the best man (tranny in pocket) at my brother's wedding pre-
cluded me form seeing the opening 2-1 win over Rochdale on a hot
August afternoon, but come the 26th October, after a 2-0 defeat at
Torquay, we lay in 23rd place. We were the worst but one club in the
football league! Then came **October 29th** and a 2-1 defeat of Wigan,
then top of the table. By the time Torquay came to the Vetch for the return fixture on November 30th we were 11th and after December 3rd
we were never out of the top six. That was a good year for the Swans
and Cardiff, both finishing in the play-off spots and then managing to
avoid playing each other. That was ominous – a Swans-Cardiff
play-off final? Police forces in six counties hastily made contingency
plans at the thought of thousands of rival fans making their way down
the M4 to Wembley. It was not to be though; the Cobblers putting pay
to Cardiff's dream. The return to paradise was akin to leaving your
box of sandwiches lying around and returning to find that not only
had someone eaten them but also shit in the box for good measure.
Well, John Frain shit in my sarnie box in the last minute of playing
time and condemned us to yet another season in the basement division of the football league.

The season of 1997-98 dawned – this time we were going to do it.
After a promising start and three different managers we finished in
20th position, the only consolation being that this was one place
above Cardiff. Some small consolation for this was a dreadful season
for both clubs compared to the euphoria of the last. Friday, 24th Octo-

ber saw us go to Yorkshire to beat hapless Doncaster 3-0, followed by a 1-0 win on Sunday, **2nd November** at Ninian Park, courtesy of a Sky Walker goal live on Sky! Thereafter we had only one win in the next 12 matches.

The 1998/99 season was very similar to that of 1994/95, a good cup run and this time we made it into the play-offs. However, a poor start saw us in 23rd place at the start of September and our new manager, John Hollins, must have wondered why on earth he headed west out of London. Then came **October 31st,** after which we lost only 3 games in the next 19. This time dreams of paradise regained remained just a dream but, like all football fans around the country, I keep the faith and hope for something better next time around. That is, while still keeping an eye out for that portentous period around late October.

Chapter 13

Come on Cymru! Revisited

If anyone was surprised of the success of Come on Cymru! it was me. No disrespect to the writers, but you just never know how these things will pan out, do you? Many people have said to me that they enjoyed certain chapters more than others and that's to be expected, I did too. If you haven't purchased the first offering – why not? If you did, you may just agree that Paul Ashley Jones's "Short Message from Carmarthen" and Eric the Red's "Do the Ayatollah" were highlights and worth re-peating. So here they are again for your reading pleasure.

A Short Message from Carmarthen

Paul Ashley-Jones

They say that a football club's most fanatical supporters often live away from the club itself. Born in Carmarthen, I've never lived in Swansea, and until recently had lived outside Wales for the last 10 years. But it hasn't stopped me supporting 'my' club. Although time and expense often mean matches are followed by Ceefax or radio, there are always occasions, such as derby games or cup-ties, when you just have to be there. This caused few problems when I was living in Leicester and when I spent four years in London. Things were a bit more difficult between 1992 and 1995, when we lived in Germany. While I would plan holidays home to coincide with as many games as possible, there were two particular occasions when I had to make specific trips back just for the game itself. The later trip was Wembley in 1994, probably the greatest day I've ever had as a Swansea fan. However, enough has been written about that match and my story concerns the first trip back, to Nuneaton Borough in November 1993.

Swansea had been very lucky to get a last-minute equaliser in the first round of the FA Cup at the Vetch. The omens for the replay were not good and I actually felt that we'd lose. I don't know why I wanted to go, but for whatever reason, I just had to be there. I flew to

Heathrow on the day of the game and arranged to meet two friends from Leicester at Nuneaton Station. We found our way to the ground and went to get tickets. You can imagine my delight to be told it was an all-ticket game and that there was no way in. They were kind enough to sell me a programme though, 'to give us something to read on the way home'. What nice people we thought! I poured my heart out to no avail, until a Swansea policeman told us to sit tight while he went to see what could be done. Now I have a lot of respect for our local police force but with only an hour to kick-off I wasn't about to hang around so I set off on a ticket search of my own. I managed to convince some local stewards that I had an appointment with the commercial manager, whose name I'd got from the programme. Once inside I managed to convince him that he had three tickets put aside for me that I'd booked earlier. I returned triumphant to my friends, waved the tickets at the programme-seller and disappeared into the local pub.

A few minutes before kick-off and I'm grabbed by the Swansea policeman on the way into the game. He was not pleased. He had found Robin Sharpe, Swansea's Chief Executive, who had managed to get three tickets for us and had spent 30 minutes in the freezing cold waiting to give them to me. I was very apologetic and made a feeble excuse about being moved on by the local force. I did write and thank Robin Sharpe afterwards but, although I shouldn't say it, the thought of a senior official freezing to death outside while we were enjoying a pint in front of a log fire still brings a smile to my face.

Of course, we lost, despite leading with an early Torpey goal. The evening had one final twist, however. Nuneaton equalised to take the game into extra time. I realised with horror that if I stayed I would miss the last train back to London, and my flight back to Germany the next morning. I had little choice but to say my goodbyes and leave. The local radio was covering the game and I heard Nuneaton's second goal in the taxi on the way to the station. Cornforth missed a penalty as I was getting out of the cab. As the train made its way to London, the irony of the situation hit me. I had travelled all that way to see the game and wouldn't know the final result until the morning papers. If I'd stayed in Germany I would at least have got the result on Sky. I didn't know whether to laugh or cry, which sums up my 15 years of following the Swans rather well, actually.

Ever since I became a father, one of the things I have always looked forward to was the thought of taking my children to the footy. I've done all the usual proud parental things. Within days of being born my two boys were signed up with the Junior Supporters' Club. Both have been kitted out in Babygros with the club badge on. True, they never fitted that well and my second son did develop a rash after wearing one, but there you go. But nothing would compare to the day my eldest son would be old enough for me to take him to actually watch my team, the team I have followed over the last 16 years, my beloved Swansea City.

As that day grew nearer I eased him in gently, taking him to the occasional Carmarthen Town game in the League of Wales. He'd enjoy watching for a while, and could then kick a ball around with the other kids when he got bored. I began to feel that he was ready for the Swans. And that's where the first seeds of doubt began to cross my mind. As I looked back over the last 16 years, I began to analyse just what following the Swans had given me. I was 15 when I was deemed old enough to travel the 30 miles from Carmarthen to home games by train, with friends. Then I could attend regularly. Prior to this I was only able to go with my father, and he worked on Saturdays. In my first full season, 1982-83, we were relegated from Division One. No games against the Liverpools and Man Uniteds next year then, but I knew we'd bounce back. We were relegated again the following year. All in all, the last 16 years have seen me witness four relegations and just the one promotion, in 1988 when we sneaked into the Division Four play-offs and beat Torquay in the final. (This was the first season of the play-offs and before the finals were played at Wembley. I couldn't get a ticket for the second leg and had to listen to the promotion on the radio.)

During this time I've watched some truly appalling football, seen my club go bankrupt, suffered 8-0 defeats at Liverpool and Monaco, and been humiliated at the hands of Bognor Regis and Nuneaton in the FA Cup. I can't even bring myself to estimate how much it has all cost me, financially or emotionally. On top of this I've had to endure the ridicule or, worse, sympathy of family and friends as we have lurched from one crisis to another. I can still see Kevin Cullis's face (remember him – former Cradley Town youth team coach and Swans manager for a bizarre week last season) when I close my eyes at night.

On top of this I am surrounded by the Welsh media who waste no opportunity to put down 'soccer' whilst giving saturation coverage to rugby at all levels.

Was I really prepared to push my own children down such a route, to put them through the pain and humiliation their father has suffered, and will no doubt continue to suffer? What about school, with all their friends supporting one Premiership club or another? Children can be so cruel and should I leave my sons open to ridicule at such a young age? Hell, yes! It will be character building (probably). And there have been good times. Victory at Wembley in the Autoglass Trophy in 1994. Away wins, including this season, at Cardiff. Knocking Bryan Robson's Middlesborough out of the FA Cup at Ayrsome Park. Anyway, after an appalling start we're going well at the moment. Settled in a play-off position, Jan Molby had Swansea playing neat, attractive football. It was with this in mind that on February 15 1997 I took my three-year-old son Jake to Vetch Field for the match against Scarborough.

We sat in the family stand, waited for kick-off and surveyed the scene. The crowd was fairly poor, due mainly to Wales's rugby game in France being on the telly. Scarborough brought 38 fans with them – Jakey counted them. Who said football can't be educational? We kicked off. 'Will there be a penalty, dad?' (Jakey has a thing about penalties.) 'We'll see,' I replied. Four minutes later and we scored from a penalty. We cheered and hugged each other. He was getting cold and I gave him my Swans scarf, the one my father had bought for me at my first game. Any lingering doubts I had about bringing him had long since vanished. The rest of the game was awful. Rumours had spread that Molby was leaving following an argument with the chairman over the failure to sign a striker from Bristol City the day before. The team played with no heart and lost to a late goal. I had seen it all before but it hurt more today. Jakey had given up on the game by half-time and was more engrossed in a Mister Men colouring book.

We made our way out after the game, listening to fans calling for the chairman's head. 'Why didn't we win, dad?' 'We don't always,' I replied, with an irony that was thankfully lost on him. 'We did score a penalty though,' he responded enthusiastically. I smiled. It was probably better this way. To see City win and believe it to be the norm would probably be worse for him in the long run. At least now he would know what to expect and maybe, sensibly, reject it outright. Perhaps he would be better off supporting Newcastle or whoever, as long as it's not rugby I wouldn't mind. But, of course, it doesn't work like that, does it? As we reached the car, still clutching his programme, he turned to me. 'I had a really nice time, dad.' The guilt overwhelmed me. 'Yes, I know you did, son. Sorry.'

Do the Ayatollah!

Phil Stead aka Eric the Red

It's the apples that does it. You can drink bitter all day long and you'll just fall asleep. You can go both ways with lager. But when you start on the apples, you're admitting to yourself that you want to lose control. And we started early that morning.

It had been a great night. We went to Chapter Arts Centre in Canton to see our mates in a band, U Thant. Two of the band have gone on to greater things. The bass player is in Catatonia, and one of the guitarists plays with the Super Furry Animals. But the man who has contributed most to Welsh culture is the singer, Rhys. He created the Ayatollah.

Rhys was watching the news on Friday night and witnessed the incredible scenes at the Ayatollah Khomeni's funeral in Iran. Thousands of Iranians were beating themselves about the heads, many with rocks, as their grievance took the form of self-inflicted pain. Looks like fun, thought Rhys, and that Friday night we were all 'doing the Ayatollah' as we danced on stage, naked but for empty tomato crates.

The van pulled up at 6am for the long trip to Lincoln. It's even longer when there are thirteen of you in the back of a fishmonger's van with nothing to sit on. I was on the cider by nine. With a tedious 0-0 draw on the pitch, you have to make your own entertainment. So with 20 minutes left, the City terracing hosted a cider-fuelled rave. Enter the criminal intelligence film crew, yeah, actual 'spotters'. What NCIS thought they were going to gain by filming the two coachloads from the supporters' club and a fish van full of students, I don't know. What they got was a clothed version of last night's gig. It was hard work but eventually the rest of the City fans caught on, and by the end there were 120 'doing the Ayatollah'.

As luck would have it, the following week took us to Hereford, always a big attraction for the nutters. And there were 4,000 there! Mainly because Chairman Rick Wright failed to get the match moved from the Sunday and told Hereford that all Cardiff fans would now boycott the fixture. Did we hell as like.

The Ayatollah, invented by Cardiff City fans, equalled by no one.

I went to the match with a bloke who is now an agent to many of the Welsh professionals. We had a few pub-stops, and at the last one I downed a pint a bit too quickly and 'felt unwell' in a hedge. It was only when I got to the match I realised I had lost my new false teeth, which I gave up as a bad job. I'd just got in when I saw people from the Lincoln match and they started doing the Ayatollah. There's a nice flat terrace at Hereford where nobody stands because you can't see the pitch. If you run up and down there slapping your head for half an hour, you soon get noticed. I heard some people whispering that I was from Kent. At least that's what it sounded like.

But people like it, and after the match a whole train of cars headed back to South Wales full of Valleys Commandos leaning out of the windows and even roof-surfing, slapping their heads at the same time. My own day out was saved when I found my teeth in the hedge. A quick swill and they were back in.

The Ayatollah routine was seen at most away games that season, 1991-92, and the final game at Peterborough was designated an Ayatollah Fancy Dress Party. So it was that 1500 blokes with tea towels on their heads headed for London Road. It was fun following Cardiff in those days and I was pleased to come 456th in the Ayatollah cross-terrace dash. A senior police officer was congratulating me on the behaviour of the City fans and apologising for expecting trouble when we saw that 30 nutters were on the pitch and trying to get the ball off Posh's tricky right-winger. He left them trailing and slotted the ball home. To everyone's astonishment, City got what they deserved and the referee allowed the goal.

The Ayatollah moved on from being a daft terrace routine and became a fully-fledged craze in 1993. Coinciding with City's most successful season in years, the media caught on and Sky's coverage of the Autoglass Trophy derby took the Ayatollah to a national audience, as did the BBC's live showing of the Manchester City cup-tie. TV and radio commentators discussed the phenomenon and the *Wales on Sunday* ran a full page with absurd computerised graphics showing readers how to 'do the Ayatollah'. *The South Wales Echo* ran a photo series of people doing the Ayatollah in different parts of the world. A terrified-looking Ryan Giggs was pictured in Corfu with his hands on his head.

The best Ayatollah performance ever came to Scunthorpe of all places. City were already promoted from Division 3 and we took over 5000 to Scunnie's brand new Meccano Stadium. Tickets were in so much demand that we were given three sides of the ground, including Scunthorpe's home end. Scunthorpe didn't dare win and we cruised to a 3-0 victory. It was a strange feeling to see thousands of people in the far north-east slapping their heads and then to think back to the Ayatollah's modest beginnings in front of less than 50 in Chapter Arts Centre.

The highlight of my career as a fan, if not the highlight of my life, came with a Wales friendly against Brazil at the Arms Park. I happen to be a sousaphone player and was an occasional member of a Cardiff street band. When I was told that the band were to perform on the pitch for the match, I took my chance. Bugger the sousa playing, I was doing the Ayatollah in the centre circle in front of 30,000 – I was playing for Wales at the Arms Park. That brought my first brush with the law. I had to audition in front of a panel of bobbies to prove that I could, in fact, play the instrument and wasn't just a drunken head-slapper. Which I was. But I could.

The second brush with the law was a bit more serious. When Chris Pike put Cardiff 1-0 up at the Vetch in the Welsh Cup, I celebrated by standing on a crash barrier and doing the Ayatollah. A snatch squad brushed aside the threat of my female companion and took me away. At first I thought they were joking, especially when I was led to the cells underneath the North Bank and heard some coppers protesting, 'You can't nick him, he was doing the Ayatollah at the Brazil game.' This was followed by a chant of, 'He ain't done nothing.' The arresting officer had some trouble explaining the reason for arrest and eventually settled for the heinous crime of 'leading the singing'. I was detained until midnight and released without charge after they studied the video evidence.

The Ayatollah routine has now become more of a badge of faith. It's the first thing that City fans do when they meet other City fans in unexpected places. Like pubs. And away games. New players are expected to pay their respects and slap their heads as soon as they step on the pitch for their debut. Performed by City fans for all sorts of things away from the ground, the Ayatollah is moving on from football and can often be seen at big Cardiff gigs in an ironic move back to its roots. It is strange to think that it's been going on now for over seven years, and even stranger to see young kids slapping their heads in the Canton Stand who have probably got no idea why they are doing it. Then again, neither have I. I just know that it was the apples that did it.

Chapter 14

You're Just a Bunch of Celts

Tony Jarman

It's not often that you get the chance to speak to someone who has experienced a game in Wales from the other side. Experienced, that is, in a truthful way. Most feedback from games comes from blind message-book comments on the Internet, which are sprinkled with falsehoods and misplaced loyalty. Tony Jarman has travelled to watch Welsh teams play on many occasions and shares with us his experiences, good and bad. The 'Come on Cymru!' team went to Oxford and spent a bloody good night in a pub with Tony.

My first experience of travelling to Wales, like that of most people, was for the traditional holiday, which was usually spent in Tenby. My memories of these days are clouded somewhat by the passage of time. Tenby seemed okay to me at the age of six, and anyway, in the sixties life wasn't that normal for anyone.

My thoughts always drift to a day's journey to get there. Now it doesn't seem to take that long these days but back then, and I do not jest, it took six hours to travel from Oxford to Tenby. Just what route my old man took and why I shall never know. As I said, you can now get to Swansea from Oxford in two hours, easy.

My father is the reason why I love football. He would travel the length and breadth of the country watching games. In 1991, just before he died, he completed his ambition of making it to all of the 92 football league grounds, old and new at the time. He would need to get his skates on again if he were still alive today, new clubs and grounds are sprouting up like nobody's business. He would have ticked off Cheltenham Town though; we went there in 1968!

The first match I went to see was at the beginning of the season when on holiday in Saundersfoot. It was 1965 and dad and I went to Swansea. The game was a pre-season friendly between the Swans and a touring team made up mostly of East Fife players as I remember. It ended 5-5. Seemed okay to me. I just liked being with my dad – I was five at this time and most five-year-olds like being with their dad. He smoked a pipe and entered into conversation with anyone, quite literally, if the topic was football.

I developed a liking for Swansea after this, and although it has diminished somewhat in recent times through bad personal experiences, I still look out for their results. And I have a claim to fame: I was at The Vetch in 1968 when they played Arsenal in the FA Cup. The attendance today is still a record – 32,000 plus.

As I grew older I developed a passion for Oxford City. Sad, eh? When I wasn't at their old ground I was heading towards the likes of Man United (no embarrassment in the seventies) and Birmingham City. The Blues are my team, and have been since 1971.

Here comes another confession: I love Ninian Park. I really can't see what the fuss is all about. I've been there on many occasions and even travelled there in early 1999 to see them triumph over Swansea City in a FAW Premiership trophy game. Cardiff won 3-2, and the Swansea City goalkeeper, Mathew Greg, was sodding dire. It was only later that I found out that the Swans had a number of injuries and Greg was replacing their normal keeper. Didn't take away from the fact that when Cardiff City went in winners at the end, I felt a small glow inside. I suppose I have also developed a soft spot for them. Maybe I'm sad; I also have a soft spot for Norwich City, Scunthorpe United, Newport AFC and Shamrock Rovers. And yes, I've seen them all play. I can spend hours on a Sunday morning looking at all the results from all the teams I like.

My proudest moment in years of watching football came in 1989 when *Shoot*, the footy mag for kids, did an exclusive on me as a football nutter! And my wife of fifteen years still loves me.

A lot of supporters view the trip to Ninian as a bit of a slippery banana. I've always said, "What's the bloody fuss?" But I can understand their concerns. I went to the FA Cup ties when Cardiff played Man City and Luton Town. I also watched them go out of the FA Cup to Bath City. All these games presented problems for the visiting supporters. Admittedly, you can't just wander about with your team's top on all the time, but I've seen many an away fan in the pubs around the ground on a Saturday. This is not something you can do at the best of times at Swansea.

Ninian Park is special. It has an incredible atmosphere at those games with a good attendance, and for Welsh Cup ties when only, say, a thousand turn out, it still holds a gloomy but interesting feel. I remember seeing them go up in 1993, when I believe 17,000 packed into the ground. How the hell 60,000 could get in there thirty years ago I will never know.

One of the saddest things I saw at Ninian was the death of Jock Stein. Everybody knew something was wrong that night. Even the Scots, drunk on victory and beer, could see that their hero was in trouble. I remember a massive crowd around him at the end of the game, and I hoped he had just fallen over in the celebrations – he hadn't and he died a short while later. It was very sad. I just knew the announcement would be he was dead when I listened to the early morning news on the way home to Oxford.

On a different level, the other sad moment that night was Swansea and Cardiff fans fighting before the game. The idiots were there to support Wales and all they wanted to do was fight each other? I sat in a pub with a mate and a number of Celtic and Rangers fans, staring in disbelief as the hordes ran up and down Westgate Street. Get that? Celtic and Rangers fans, together. Swansea and Cardiff fans fighting. Wales v Scotland, the winner goes to a major final, Scotland deserved to win on that alone.

It can be a bit nasty at Ninian Park and equally at The Vetch Field. My mates believe that it is down to the fact that the Welsh see themselves as inferior to the English, which is why whenever they travel they have to prove something. I can't disagree with this, is there any other explanation?

Whenever I get the chance I'm off to a game, rarely with my wife these days, she leaves me to get on with it. My mate Peter, a policeman from Oxford, tags along most times and he does enjoy our days out. He came along to Ninian Park in 1993 for the Cardiff v Swansea game just before Christmas. It was my first Welsh derby game. I left with twenty minutes to go. It was like a war. Fighting on the pitch, in the stands, outside the ground. Police horses everywhere. It was my worst experience of football violence. I hated it. Cardiff won 1-0, and

for years after the fans of both clubs were banned from the away fixture. These days they are bussed in, 2000 Swansea fans the last time
to Ninian. What a waste of police resources! Having said that I honestly believe it is a lifesaving measure. If it had been allowed to go on I
reckon people could have been killed. In fact, I would have put large
amounts of cash on it. That Welsh derby was my first and last, it
frightened me silly.

In my humble opinion Welsh football is bigger now than it has
been for many years. Attendances are up massively at Swansea and
Cardiff, I can't speak for Wrexham, but South Wales is experiencing a
revival. Cardiff City going up to the Second Division at the end of
1999 was a boon. Swansea should have made it – they have a good
manager but never seem to spend the extra cash that would secure
them promotion. I think they may make it this time around, though. If
they did and Cardiff stayed up, Welsh football could be huge. The
support of both Cardiff and Swansea is very large; they have a big
pulling area. It should happen. I do worry about the consequences for
football, however. But perhaps in better stadia with improved levels
of football both sets of fans would behave.

I've been at games when the country thing, Wales v England,
seems to take over. The Man City FA Cup tie was definitely England v
Wales. This, of course, provokes increased violence, it's bound to.
The English see it as an opportunity to prove that they are better, the
Welsh just won't have it at any level. Cardiff City fans are renowned
for their nationalistic pride and I respect them for that. This is less
true of Swansea, but both have real problems at times. It's sad to see
games deteriorate.

I went to Reading v Cardiff a few years back, again in the FA Cup.
At the time Jason Bowen was a Reading player and the Cardiff fans
chanted "You Jack bastard" at him. Reading fans thought they were
singing something else at their black centre forward Carl Asaba. I explained to furious Reading supporters around me in the stand that
they were misunderstood, and got a punch in the gob for being a
sheep-shagger! The problem I had here was I couldn't explain I was
from Oxford, they would have killed me!

The more important problem, however, is that there will always be

Swansea City fans on the pre-season tour of Ireland 1999.

games like these. I'm a genuine football fan and in this situation I suffered the most. But like the proverbial lemming, I keep going.

English supporters do see any game against a Welsh team as an opportunity for nationalistic pride to surface. I've seen many a plastic sheep waved at both Cardiff and Swansea fans. In recent times they have joined in the chants of "Sheep-shaggers" and brought their own sheep, a brilliant response, and maybe the best one. It shut up Swindon fans when Cardiff went there in the FA Cup – another game I would find it hard to explain to anyone where I live.

My funniest moment as a football fan was at a Reading v Swansea game about seven years ago. Before the game my wife, Peter and his current girlfriend had a few pints in the pub at the railway station in Reading. Swansea fans, already causing problems, were arriving in hordes. A group of about twenty came into the pub. Pete wanted away, and I could see he was afraid of what may happen. I insisted we were no target for them. After about five minutes two of the group came over to us. One asked how far the ground was. I said it was a fair walk. This chap was eating from a bag of chips. He looked at me and

Tony dreams of Welsh football, the North Bank Swansea.

my wife and said in a broad Welsh accent, and I will never forget this, "You Reading then?"

I replied we were not and just there for the game. It did not register at all. He consumed another chip, stepped back and said, "You want some?" He was gesturing with both hands. Peter's girlfriend said, "Don't mind if I do," and took a chip from his bag. He looked so stupid even his mate laughed. I told him that in no way did we want some or anymore, we finished our drinks and left. I later saw him scaling the floodlight pylon in the ground as once again the Welsh support brought disgrace on their club and country.

There are generally more happy memories than bad. I've made a number of very good friends who follow Cardiff and have been saved by many more. I've received lifts, to my door no less, on two occasions from saintly Cardiff fans – after breaking down coming away from games in Cambridge and Swindon. I've bloody cried when the Cardiff faithful were in full song at three games at least. They are magnificent when all they want is for Cardiff to win. I met Keith, the author of this book, in the toilets at West Ham v Swansea City (sorry, Keith!). His mates, all Swans fans from England, are the reason why I love football so much. Where he finds the time to do what he does, and the quantity, I will never know. The best Jack in the world. That's all you're getting, Keith. He has devoted his life to football; he deserves so much more from football in return. Like all fans he gets nothing but pride when his team wins. But perhaps this is payment enough.

Whenever I go to Cardiff, a lovely place, I always book in to a B&B in Cathedral Road. My wife loves the shops. I love the atmosphere. The city-centre pubs are excellent for a few jars on any day of the week, including match days. Whenever I go I make a weekend of it, travelling around the area to the Vale of Glamorgan and sometimes down to West Wales. When I do these obscure things I always view the football grounds of the towns I visit. I was amazed to see Inter Cardiff's ground off the carriageway on the way into the city and I've also had a packed lunch at Cwmbran's impressive stadium. One of the staff asked me if I was mad, I couldn't respond.

Another ground just off a carriageway is Haverfordwest's. I held up the traffic when I spotted it three years back on another Welsh pilgrimage. Looking down from the road, I felt I just had to have a closer look. The first problem was getting to it; I just couldn't find the road downwards! Eventually I parked in a local supermarket, skipped a few hedges and had a walk on the pitch. Haverfordwest County are also The Bluebirds, The Bluebirds of West Wales no less, and they have an impressive stand and club to boot. If only more of us could see what these smaller Welsh clubs have to offer. Maybe it's only a last season for a well-known pro giving up the game, or a youngster who can't cut it at the bigger clubs, but all of you should have a look. If it's your cup of tea that is.

Best cup of tea? Rochdale.

Worst? Macclesfield.

Best Pie? Hearts.

Worst? Metz. Don't go there, it smells.

Of course, I have also completed the 92 grounds, up to date and all. All right, dad? I know a bloke who collects and photographs corner flags. I know another who photographs turnstiles. I have a badge from all the clubs I have visited, have you? I'm sad.

I get along to about fifty games a year, that's January to January. I've been to two World Cups, two Euro Championships and over 100 internationals. I've seen Swansea City play 14 times and Cardiff City 56 times, not that I'm counting. I love the passion, I hate the violence. The feeling of being in a foreign country is addictive.

Strange? Not as strange as Cowdenbeath v Motherwell or Bayern V BMG maybe, but the Welsh thing inspired me. They have their music and their culture. It's often misunderstood, often hated, but they have it in abundance. They have identity and passion, the thing which football thrives on, that keeps me going. And go I will, it's so different from anything else. It's been good. Thank you.

Postscript: *Tony Jarman continues to watch football all over the world and his wife still loves him.*

Chapter 15

Just for a Laugh

Keith Haynes

Welsh football fans, like thousands all over all over the world, are fiercely competitive and given to making exaggerated claims for their clubs. Have a browse through these facts and figures from the past sixty years or so for the three Welsh teams in the English league system. I think you may find some solace no matter which team you support. These results and figures do not include The Welsh Cup, FAW Premier Cup, or European Competition.

Let's start here, Cardiff City have played in Europe more times than The Swans, but when Swansea City play Cardiff City the results are often very close. Since 1929, records show that Swansea and Cardiff have met in the FA Cup, League Cup and Football League on 53 occasions. Many of us have witnessed these classic encounters. When Swansea City were in what is now the Premiership they played Cardiff City in the Welsh Cup. You would, of course, have expected the Swans to have eased through in this fixture. But expectations are often overturned in these fixtures! In recent times, with the odd exception, the clubs are inseparable. Have a look at this record since 1929:

	Swansea City Wins	Cardiff City Wins	Draws
League:	18	16	14
FA Cup:	1	0	0
League Cup:	2	2	0
Total	21	18	14

The dispute's not settled yet though because off the pitch Cardiff City can claim certain victories in the fluctuating attendance figures. Cardiff's best recorded attendance playing league opposition is 57,893 for a game against Arsenal in April 1953. Swansea City's best is against the same club in 1968. 32,796 packed into the Vetch for a FA Cup tie.

To me, events on the pitch matter most, and those statistics are here for all to see. But then I am a Jack!

Let's move it on a bit. Cardiff City's highest fee paid for a player is £180,000 for one Godfrey Ingram from the infamous San Jose Earthquakes. Swansea City can boast payment of £340,000 to Liverpool for the ill-fated Colin Irwin in 1981. Highest fees received are £300,000 in Cardiff's case for Nathan Blake when he moved to Sheffield United in 1994. He should have gone for a lot more money, but isn't that always the case? Swansea City sold Des Lyttle to Nottingham Forest for £375,000 in 1993. But does receiving or paying a higher fee make you a better club? Or having a higher attendance figure for that matter?

The amazing statistic is that neither club has ever done a league double over the other in one season. Swansea City have come close in the past few years, but from the 48 league games played to the end of 1999 no team had managed the elusive double.

So how about internationals then? Cardiff City's case is with Alf Sherwood, who played in 39 internationals for Wales. Swansea City can turn to Ivor Allchurch, who played on 42 occasions for his country. Ivor Allchurch also scored on 166 occasions for the Swans, Cardiff's Len Davies scored on 128.

Gate receipts are interesting, has anyone noticed how some clubs' gate receipts are dated to years back? Swansea City state that their biggest gate receipts date back to 1982. Apparently £36,477 was taken on the gates that day for a game against Liverpool. Cardiff City smash this record easily, taking £141,756 for the FA Cup tie against Manchester City in 1994. Interestingly enough, both Swansea City and Cardiff City won these games.

But did Swansea not secure massive receipts from the Wembley Final appearances of 1994 and 1997? And, of course, in both cases there would have been other revenues like TV money. £80,000 is up for grabs for a team playing a league game on SKY TV. Don't believe any other figures, this is a fact. When the teams have met on SKY TV all the fixtures have been at Ninian Park. The Autoglass tie screened in the early nineties saw a Swansea victory after extra time. Later, in 1998, Keith Walker blasted in the winner for a 1-0 Swansea victory. In 1999 both teams fought out a 0-0 draw.

So where do we go from here? Highest scoring wins? Okay, Cardiff

City's biggest cup win was 8-0 v Enfield in 1931. Swansea City's is recorded as 12-0 against Sliema Wanderers in 1981. The European Cup Winners' Cup I know, but worthy of a mention and nearly a European record.

Cardiff City can delight in Swansea City's loss at Anfield in the FA Cup in 1990. Liverpool won 8-0 that night after a 0-0 draw at the Vetch Field. Of course, having said that may I remind you of Cardiff City's 11-2 loss against Sheffield United?

How about the most goals scored in a league season? Swansea Town as they were then have Cyril Pearce, who in 1931/32 blasted in 35 Goals for the Swans. Stan Richards replied in 1946/47 with 30 for Cardiff City.

Phil Dwyer made 471 appearances for Cardiff City; Wilfred Milne 585 for Swansea. I don't think even Roger Freestone will match these figures

Cardiff City have won the Welsh Cup more times than Swansea. It goes on and on. And it's fun.

Swansea and Cardiff – the facts

Here are the recorded scores of Swansea City/Town v Cardiff City since 1929. In here you will see some amazing games, some you will remember: John Buchanan's last-minute tap in from 40 odd yards in 1980, to equalise in the Christmas derby game at Ninian, or Jimmy Gilligan's FA Cup effort that secured a Swansea City victory in 1991 at The Vetch. Massive moments. Here are the facts.

English Division 3	Cardiff City	0-0	Swansea City	18-04-1999
English Division 3	Swansea City	2-1	Cardiff City	22-11-1998
English Division 3	Swansea City	1-1	Cardiff City	08-03-1998
English Division 3	Cardiff City	0-1	Swansea City	02-11-1997
English Division 3	Swansea City	0-1	Cardiff City	02-03-1997
English Division 3	Cardiff City	1-3	Swansea City	03-12-1996
English Division 2	Swansea City	4-1	Cardiff City	07-03-1995
English Division 2	Cardiff City	1-1	Swansea City	06-09-1994
English Division 2	Swansea City	1-0	Cardiff City	02-04-1994
English Division 2	Cardiff City	1-0	Swansea City	22-12-1993
English FA Cup	Swansea City	2:1	Cardiff City	16-11-1991
English Division 3 (old)	Cardiff City	0-2	Swansea City	16-04-1990

English Division 3 (old)	Swansea City	0-1	Cardiff City	26-12-1989
English Division 3 (old)	Swansea City	1–1	Cardiff City	27-03-1989
English Division 3 (old)	Cardiff City	2-2	Swansea City	26-12-1988
English League Cup	Swansea City	0-2	Cardiff City	20-09-1988
English League Cup	Cardiff City	0-1	Swansea City	30-08-1988
English Division 4	Swansea City	2-2	Cardiff City	01-01-1988
English Division 4	Cardiff City	1-0	Swansea City	29-08-1987
English Division 4	Swansea City	2-0	Cardiff City	20-04-1987
English Division 4	Cardiff City	0-0	Swansea City	26-12-1986
English Division 3 (old)	Swansea City	2-0	Cardiff City	31-03-1986
English Division 3 (old)	Cardiff City	1-0	Swansea City	26-12-1985
English League Cup	Swansea City	3-1	Cardiff City	03-09-1985
English League Cup	Cardiff City	2-1	Swansea City	20-08-1985
English Division 2 (old)	Swansea City	3-2	Cardiff City	21-04-1984
English Division 2 (old)	Cardiff City	3-2	Swansea City	26-12-1983
English Division 2 (old)	Swansea City	1-1	Cardiff City	18-04-1981
English Division 2 (old)	Cardiff City	3-3	Swansea City	27-12-1980
English Division 2 (old)	Cardiff City	1-0	Swansea City	07-04-1980
English Division 2 (old)	Swansea City	2-1	Cardiff City	01-01-1980
English Division 2 (old)	Cardiff City	5-0	Swansea City	06-04-1965
English Division 2 (old)	Swansea City	3-2	Cardiff City	26-12-1964
English Division 2 (old)	Swansea City	3-0	Cardiff City	28-03-1964
English Division 2 (old)	Cardiff City	1-1	Swansea City	19-10-1963
English Division 2 (old)	Cardiff City	5-2	Swansea City	15-09-1962
English Division 2 (old)	Swansea City	2-1	Cardiff City	04-09-1962
English Division 2 (old)	Swansea City	3-3	Cardiff City	28-03-1960
English Division 2 (old)	Cardiff City	2-1	Swansea City	07-11-1959
English Division 2 (old)	Swansea City	1-3	Cardiff City	15-04-1959
English Division 2 (old)	Cardiff City	0-1	Swansea City	07-03-1959
English Division 2 (old)	Swansea City	0-1	Cardiff City	21-12-1957
English Division 2 (old)	Cardiff City	0-0	Swansea City	24-08-1957
English Division 2 (old)	Cardiff City	3-0	Swansea City	26-12-1951
English Division 2 (old)	Swansea City	1-1	Cardiff City	25-12-1951
English Division 2 (old)	Cardiff City	1-0	Swansea City	24-03-1951
English Division 2 (old)	Swansea City	1-0	Cardiff City	04-11-1950
English Division 2 (old)	Swansea City	5-1	Cardiff City	24-12-1949
English Division 2 (old)	Cardiff City	1-0	Swansea City	27-08-1949
English Division 2 (old)	Cardiff City	1-0	Swansea City	27-12-1930
English Division 2 (old)	Swansea City	3-2	Cardiff City	30-08-1930
English Division 2 (old)	Swansea City	1-0	Cardiff City	08-02-1930
English Division 2 (old)	Cardiff City	0-0	Swansea City	05-10-1929

What about Wrexham?

Wrexham fans would argue that they have had the best of the results. They have won against Swansea City more times than they have lost but their record against Cardiff City is poor. Swansea have nearly always struggled at The Racecourse; in fact, overall they have only beaten Wrexham on eight occasions. Wrexham have recorded 13 wins with six draws.

Cardiff City have found games against Wrexham very appealing indeed. Take the 1991/92 season. Cardiff beat Wrexham 3-0 at The Racecourse and hammered them 5-0 at Ninian. In 1994 Cardiff enjoyed another massive victory, winning 5-1, again at Ninian Park. These fixtures may not provoke the passion of a Welsh derby game but they matter a lot to the fans of both teams. Wrexham have also seen some excellent victories over their rivals from the south. In 1986 Wrexham beat The Bluebirds 5-1 at The Racecourse in the old Fourth Division. In 1977 Cardiff City knocked Wrexham out of the FA Cup in a thriller ending 3-2 in favour of the home team. Some have said that this was the finest game of cup football seen at Ninian in many years.

Looking deeper, the record books show Wrexham receiving £800,000 from Birmingham City in 1997 for Bryan Hughes. Tom Bamford hammered home 175 goals for the club, and recorded 44 goals in one season in 1933/34. Arfon Griffiths played for Wrexham between 1959 and 1979. Yes, twenty years covered his 592 appearances. Remarkable!

In 1962 Wrexham hammered Hartlepool United 10-1 in a league game. Hartlepool have also suffered in the south when Swansea City hammered them 8-0 in the old Fourth Division in 1978. These are amazing statistics. Those that witnessed these games must have realised that they were seeing history in the making. A traditional football hammering is 5-1, but 10-1? Of course, let's not forget Wrexham's 9-0 defeat at Brentford in a Third Division game or, indeed, their 6-0 humiliation of Charlton Athletic in an FA Cup game in 1980.

Cardiff v Wrexham

Here are the recorded results of Wrexham's games against both Cardiff City and Swansea City.

English Division 2	Cardiff City	1-1	Wrexham	20-08-1999
English Division 2	Wrexham	0-3	Cardiff City	18-03-1995
English Division 2	Cardiff City	0-0	Wrexham	30-08-1994
English Division 2	Cardiff City	5-1	Wrexham	05-02-1994
English Division 2	Wrexham	3-1	Cardiff City	23-10-1993
English Division 3	Wrexham	0-2	Cardiff City	17-04-1993
English Division 3	Cardiff City	1-2	Wrexham	18-12-1992
English Division 4	Wrexham	0-3	Cardiff City	25-04-1992
English Division 4	Cardiff City	5-0	Wrexham	05-10-1991
English Division 4	Wrexham	1-0	Cardiff City	22-03-1991
English Division 4	Cardiff City	1-0	Wrexham	05-10-1990
English Division 4	Cardiff City	1-1	Wrexham	16-03-1988
English Division 4	Wrexham	3-0	Cardiff City	12-09-1987
English Division 4	Cardiff City	0-0	Wrexham	21-03-1987
English Division 4	Wrexham	5-1	Cardiff City	11-10-1986
English Division 3 (old)	Wrexham	0-0	Cardiff City	15-01-1983
English Division 3 (old)	Cardiff City	1-2	Wrexham	28-08-1982
English Division 2 (old)	Wrexham	3-1	Cardiff City	24-11-1981
English Division 2 (old)	Cardiff City	3-2	Wrexham	04-11-1981
English Division 2 (old)	Wrexham	1-0	Cardiff City	12-11-1980
English Division 2 (old)	Cardiff City	0-1	Wrexham	19-08-1980
English Division 2 (old)	Cardiff City	1-0	Wrexham	12-01-1980
English Division 2 (old)	Wrexham	0-1	Cardiff City	01-09-1979
English Division 2 (old)	Cardiff City	1-0	Wrexham	14-05-1979
English Division 2 (old)	Wrexham	1-2	Cardiff City	30-09-1978
English FA Cup	Cardiff City	3-2	Wrexham	29-01-1977
English Division 3 (old)	Wrexham	1-1	Cardiff City	08-03-1976
English Division 3 (old)	Cardiff City	3-0	Wrexham	04-10-1975
English League Cup	Cardiff City	3-0	Wrexham	01-10-1963
English League Cup	Wrexham	1-1	Cardiff City	
English League Cup	Cardiff City	2-2	Wrexham	

Swansea City v. Wrexham

English Division 2	Swansea City	1-3	Wrexham	06-04-1996
English Division 2	Wrexham	1-0	Swansea City	28-10-1995
English Division 2	Swansea City	0-0	Wrexham	04-02-1995
English Division 2	Wrexham	4-1	Swansea City	26-11-1994

English Division 2	Wrexham	3-2	Swansea City	11-12-1993
English Division 2	Swansea City	3-1	Wrexham	21-08-1993
English Division 4	Wrexham	1-2	Swansea City	12-03-1988
English Division 4	Swansea City	2-1	Wrexham	10-10-1987
English Division 4	Swansea City	0-3	Wrexham	02-05-1987
English Division 4	Wrexham	0-0	Swansea City	29-11-1986
English Division 2 (old)	Swansea City	3-1	Wrexham	06-03-1981
English Division 2 (old)	Wrexham	1-1	Swansea City	04-10-1980
English Division 2 (old)	Swansea City	1-0	Wrexham	12-04-1980
English Division 2 (old)	Wrexham	1-0	Swansea City	01-12-1979
English Division 3 (old)	Wrexham	1-0	Swansea City	07-04-1973
English Division 3 (old)	Swansea City	3-1	Wrexham	01-12-1972
English Division 3 (old)	Wrexham	2-0	Swansea City	29-04-1972
English Division 3 (old)	Swansea City	0-2	Wrexham	11-04-1972
English Division 3 (old)	Wrexham	1-1	Swansea City	09-01-1971
English Division 3 (old)	Swansea City	3-0	Wrexham	29-09-1970
English Division 4	Wrexham	1-1	Swansea City	14-03-1970
English Division 4	Swansea City	1-2	Wrexham	17-02-1970
English Division 4	Wrexham	2-0	Swansea City	07-10-1978
English Division 4	Swansea City	0-0	Wrexham	27-08-1968
English Division 4	Wrexham	2-1	Swansea City	20-01-1968
English Division 4	Swansea City	2-0	Wrexham	16-09-1967
English F A Cup	Wrexham	2-1	Swansea City	

Lots of facts, lots of arguments. Show a football fan a fact that their team lost 8-0 and they will tell you a positive, guaranteed.

▸ Swansea City lost 8-0 at Anfield! Yeah, but we took 5,000 fans there and one of them scored a goal!

▸ Cardiff City lost 4-1 at Swansea! Yeah, but it was snowing and the result didn't matter that much, anyway, our rivals are Bristol City!

▸ Swansea City lost at home to Cardiff! Yeah, but that's the only time they have beaten us in five years!

▸ Wrexham had five goals put past them by Cardiff again! Yeah, but we are always above them in the league, and anyway our rivals are Chester City not Cardiff.

You have read the facts, make of them what you will. They refer in the main to English competition, the Welsh Cup tells a different story ... Maybe next time.

Chapter 16

From Flowers in the Dustbin to Roses in the Garden

Keith Haynes

"Flowers in the Dustbin" was the final article in the first edition of *Come on Cymru!* – I thought that it reflected the attitude of the time. Both Swansea and Cardiff were in the doldrums and Wrexham were again struggling. However, a year is a long time in football, maybe those rotting flowers are now turning into roses, or, indeed, daffodils.

All football fans look at their own clubs and then compare their position with their closest rivals. The supporters of Cardiff City and Swansea City seem to do this on a daily basis. Transfer fees, league position, attendances, whatever... Both sides will claim victory for even the most inconsequential fact.

Cardiff City now sit proudly amongst the fixtures for the Second Division for the year 2000. Swansea City, if they have the vision they claim to have, will join them next season. That is if the share holders of the plc that holds the purse strings just hang on for a few moments and give Neil McClure the chance to prove a few points. It's a long shot that one. Swansea will have new faces on the pitch this season. The fans will not be happy with

Forward thinking? Steve Hamer and John Hollins with the traditional Morfa stadium plans at another press conference. 1999/2000 – a watershed season for Swansea City?

players leaving, especially if those players should form a part of a championship-winning squad. Behind the scenes there is a definite reluctance on the part of manager John Hollins to get out there and look at the talent that is available. I've said before that he has done well with the players he has, but he has to do better. Three wins better, it's not a lot. Swansea City can do it.

Cardiff City could easily be in the First Division by June 2000. Do I really need to say any more? They must take this chance. Imagine Cardiff City in the First Division, just twelve months away from The Premiership? Are you laughing? Then you are foolish, just look where Watford and Bradford City are now. It can be done.

Wrexham can join them – they have a splendid new stand and a careful chairman who doesn't revel in pie-in-the-sky tabloid comments, unlike some. He is a Wrexham fan and has very slowly moved the club closer to security and, indeed, success.

The League of Wales will only have its day in Europe. But these teams can humiliate anyone on their day. Barry Town's success is well documented, and that's what football is all about – the Barry Towns of this world.

Barry Town lift the Welsh Cup after defeating Cardiff City. They have gone on to dominate Welsh club football.

We now have a new manager for the Welsh national team. Gould tried his best and he failed, but at least he put his heart on his sleeve, albeit foolishly at times. We look towards World Cup qualification.

The stories you have read in _Come on Cymru!_ and in this offering are stories we all relate to, no matter where we watch from or which team we support. Of course, you will disagree at times but we can't all agree on everything, that would make supporting football very boring indeed. It's time, though, that the people who run our clubs realised that we are not thick idiots with scarves tied around our wrists, singing foul songs about kicking heads in. We can see through their tales and diatribe, we can form our own opinions. They would love to be able to box us all off in the hooligan bin, that way they know what the supporter is, but it's not possible. It never has been.

Supporters these days see exactly what is going on at their club. A moment's foolishness by a chairman results in months of hatred from the terraces. Surely these intelligent people can see that? Surely they don't think they can lie to people with greater knowledge of the game than their own?

If the powers that be continue to think that by bluffing and stuttering through their lives they will reach their goal then the Welsh game and the game in general will suffer. The Welsh fixtures at Anfield just may have cost us the long-term objective of qualifying for the European Championships. Just maybe, it's a point.

The situation is now clear, the supporters hold the key. They make the decision on whether to go to see their teams play or not and their money is badly needed by all. They not only pay the turnstile operator, they buy the shirts, the T-shirts, the other merchandise, and they spread the word. Yes, the supporters of tomorrow come from the parents of today.

Clubs have to do more to gather these individuals together and nurture their support, so that one day they will bring others, and they, in turn, will bring others to the grounds of Wales. More support for our teams. All three Welsh clubs have massive support, remember we represent a nation not a county or a town. That support is vital if they are to climb the ladder and bring back some glory to the Welsh game. The powers that be have to do more; they have to act now.

Why don't they consider free entry for under 5s? Or half-price admis-

The new face of Welsh derby football. Fans bussed to games and a host of police to keep them apart.

... *and the way it used to be.*

sion for one or two midweek games that don't have the lure of Cup tickets attached to them? Just the normal fixture for the normal fan to attend. Just a thought. Maybe even a more proactive approach from the players is needed; a few more hours with the kids and a few more hearts will be won. There are many ideas that offer potential solutions.

But things are rosier than two years ago. The millennium offers us an optimistic threshold. We can look far further forward now than when we were embroiled in the violent side of things in the seventies and eighties. We still have violence, far too much and far too often at Swansea and Cardiff games. The picture here of coaches being brought in to bus everyone to the South Wales derby is absurd in this day and age. Not even Rangers and Celtic suffer these problems, but we do. The violent elements at both clubs continue to hinder the normal fan and the family enclosures have also seen violence in recent years. Is it in our natural make-up? Are we just fighting back because of years of neglect? If the answer is yes then why do we fight each other? Why can't Swansea and Cardiff fans watch their national side in peace?

Why do football fans fight at all? If anyone has the answer then please let someone know, a financially assured future awaits you. Of course, there isn't just one answer. Sanitising grounds by making them all-seater doesn't work at Chelsea so it won't work at Swansea. Visiting supporters to both Cardiff and Swansea are very much in the minority these days, they know the journey and the reception isn't worth the hassle. And from what I saw last season I don't blame them.

I stood at the front of the seated area at Glanford Park, Scunthorpe with some 1,800 Swans fans on a mild summer's evening in May 99. It was the play-off semi-final second leg. Only Welsh fans could produce the atmosphere that night. The idiot from the Scunthorpe dressing room who ran on to the pitch and gave an England flag to Scunthorpe supporters right next to Swansea fans should no longer be employed as a coach or whatever he was. This is where clubs like Scunthorpe will always be clubs like Scunthorpe. They may have their moment of glory but that's all it will be. We in Wales deserve and will have more.

People who don't understand football run these clubs and they would have been responsible if that stupid moment of enticement had resulted in a riot. But would the football league have seen it like that? We all have our responsibilities, and that includes the supporters, players and every last soul attached to a club. Idiots like the Scunthorpe flag carrier should be excluded from the game as quickly as any hooligan. I hope he reads this, I cannot think of anything he can say in his defence for this act of stupidity.

The situation really remains as it was two years, ten years, fifty years ago. Football supporters are passionate people, but they know what's right and what's wrong and they also know when something needs changing.

We end this book on a positive note but with many notes of caution. It's looking better, in fact, it's getting better all the time. I hope that the future of the game rewards you with fulfilled hopes and dreams for your club, no matter the level or the team. As I said before, no matter the colour, no matter the club, let's keep it there. Forever.

Come on Cymru!

Chapter 17

Keeping in Touch with Football in Wales

Some of you may want to know more about the game, and even keep up to speed on the latest developments from the fans' point of view. There are a host of fanzines available at very reasonable prices. They offer a good insight into the clubs they support, or at times don't support. The ones listed here are just a selection of magazines and fanzines available at this time. All the fanzines listed require your support. You will get a reply and they may print your views. Support them, they deserve it.

Remember that you may also be able to influence the everyday running of your club by offering your opinions on the way it is run. They won't always be happy to hear from you but they will listen, and you never know you may even get a response.

Welsh Football Magazine

For an overall view of football in Wales, "Welsh Football" magazine can be contacted at 57 Thornhill Road, Cardiff CF14 6PE. Readers of *Come on Cymru 2000* can take out a NEW subscription until the end of the 1999-2000 season and will receive the first issue free. Invoice sent with first issue. Or send for the latest issue (£2 plus 30p p&p).

On the Net

It's easy these days to keep up with the Welsh sides via the Internet. Just type your club's name into any search engine and you are away. Links from all sites are a good way to get around. All the main Welsh clubs and many more have a whole host of sites that will offer many opinions on the game in Wales. The sections in this book by Gary Martin, Michael Morris and Rhys Gwynllyw should give you some idea of what to expect, but there are many more.

Check out any links page and you will reveal the many hundreds of web sites that accommodate Welsh football.

Cardiff City

The club's postal address is Cardiff City AFC, Ninian Park, Cardiff, South Glamorgan

"Watch the Bluebirds Fly", 10 King St, Abercynon, Mid Glamorgan CF45 4UW

"The Thin Blue Line", PO BOX 265, Cardiff CF2 3YH

Swansea City

The club's postal address is Swansea City AFC, The Vetch Field, Swansea, West Glamorgan

"Jackanory", PO BOX 372, Swansea SA1 6YY

"Mouthful of Lead", 30 Cadrawd Rd, Townhill, Swansea SA1 6UG

Wrexham AFC

The club's postal address is Wrexham AFC, The Racecourse, Wrexham, Clwyd

"The Sheeping Giant", 21 Dolafon, Pen-i-Bont Fawr, Nr Oswestry SY10 0PA

"Red Passion", 139 Laund Rd, Salendine Nook, Huddersfield HD3 3TZ

The Welsh League and the national team

"Bring me the head of Alun Evans", 78 Slater St, Warrington, WA4 1DW

"A470", 22 Stanley Avenue, Valley, Ynys Mon LL65 3BD

Aberystwyth Town FC

"Linesman, you're rubbish", Holly Dene, Caradole Rd, Aberystwyth, Dyfed SY23 2LB

Barry Town FC

"38 Hours from Vilnius", Celtic View, Harbour Rd, Barry CF62 5SA

Caernarfon Town FC

"The Oval Ball", Rhianfa, Station Rd, Llanrug, Caernarfon

Colwyn Bay FC

Flat 2, Erskine Rd, Colwyn Bay, LL29 8EU

Merthyr AFC

"Dial 'M' for Merthyr", 109 Bryrunair Rd, Godreaman, Merthyr CF44 6NB

"Tiny Taff's Adventures", 20 Bro Dawel, Merthyr CF47 0YT

"The Brecon Road Beat", 95a Lakeside Gardens, Merthyr, Mid Glamorgan

Newport AFC

"Run Lads, Shoot Lads", 10 Grosvenor Rd, Bassaleg, Newport, Gwent NP1 9PY

SWANSEA CITY FOOTBALL CLUB

Support The Swans!

Swansea City AFC
Vetch Field, Swansea SA1 3SU

Main office: 01792 544444; Ticket hotline: 0870 131912
Swanline: 0891 542123; Club shop: 01792 462584
E-mail: swans.prom@btinternet.com

CARDIFF CITY AFC

Aim high with The Bluebirds

Cardiff City AFC
Sloper Road
Cardiff CF1 8SX

Tel: (01222) 221001

Email: ccafc@baynet.co.uk

Cardiff City are stockists of *Come on Cymru!*

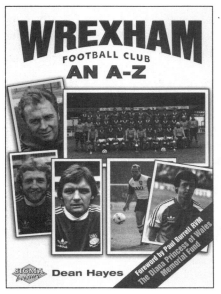

WREXHAM FC: An A-Z
Dean Hayes

Followers of Wrexham, this is the book for you! This new book is packed with stories, facts and figures all arranged alphabetically for easy reference, so that virtually any question about the Robins can be authoritatively answered. There are almost 300 entries in this A-Z including biographies of players and managers who have made important contributions over the years. Packed with photographs of old, new and little-known stories, this is one of the most accessible reference books on the subject. *£6.95*

FOOTBALL & WAR

Gerard Reid

When at war, supporters identify with their 'side' for reasons as diverse as class, religion, and patriotism. Sound familiar? In football, supporters' beliefs can result in conflicts that go far deeper than the actual 'game'. These are the games that this book is about. Chapters include: games where nations were in actual conflict (Argentina v England, and England v Ireland), and even games which were the direct cause of war (Honduras v El Salvador). This is the first book to explore this subject. *£6.95*